SPARKLE AND GROW

A Personal Growth Strategy Guide
for Influencers Living in a Digital World

By Jamie Wilkinson

Sparkle and Grow: A Personal Growth Strategy for Influencers Living in a Digital World
Copyright © 2024 by Jamie Wilkinson

This book is a work of nonfiction. The information provided is based on the author's experiences, research, and opinions. The author and publisher make no representations or warranties with respect to the accuracy or completeness of the contents of this book and disclaim any implied warranties of fitness for a particular purpose. The advice and strategies contained herein may not be suitable for every situation. Readers should use their discretion when applying the information provided in this book.

Published by Jamie Wilkinson
Printed in the United States of America

Printed and Distributed by Lulu Press, Inc.

ISBN: 978-1-300-88436-1
Cover Design: Jamie Wilkinson

For more information, visit www.sparkleandgrow.com

Grow Through the Sparkles

Sparkle 1: Introduction – The Power of Influence

In the hustle of today's online world, the superpower of influence is beyond comparison. Whether you're a personal brand, small business owner, or a full-time influencer, you have an incredible opportunity to shape perceptions, build relationships, and impact lives. But here's the truth: none of this matters if you aren't taking care of *yourself*. Your personal wellbeing is not just an accessory to your online marketing strategy—it's the foundation. If your mindset isn't in the right place, even the most flawless, technically-sound social media strategy will crumble.

It doesn't matter how perfect your Instagram feed looks, how well you understand algorithms, or how great your product or service is—without confidence and authenticity, your growth will stall. Those are the *real* tools that will catapult you to the next level, and they are the very heart of what we're diving into in this book. But let me be crystal clear: this is not just another fluffy, feel-good, motivational read that gives you a temporary high. I'm not here to make you feel a little better for a few weeks, only to find yourself in the exact same place months later. This book is designed to truly *transform* you, but only if you're willing to put in the work.

This is not a passive journey. Each chapter of this book contains real, tangible assignments that are designed to push you. These aren't optional "nice to haves"—they're essential steps if you want to push yourself and your social media presence to the next level. This book is about growing both you *and* your social media presence—if you let it. There's no magic in just reading these words; the real magic lies in the *action* you take afterward. The formula is simple: the more you act, the more you grow. Even taking the "*wrong*" action will propel you forward. Why? Because failure provides you with priceless data. You'll learn what doesn't work, and that knowledge is like a compass guiding you in the right direction.

When you think about it, every piece of content you share is like planting a seed. Sometimes it will blossom immediately, and other times it might need more nurturing. But without planting anything, you can't expect growth. The same goes for action in your life and career—action, even imperfect, is what separates those who succeed from those who stand still, trapped by fear.

No matter what your niche is—whether you're selling products, services, or even ideas—being an influencer in today's world comes with a big responsibility. This isn't just about promoting the next big thing or chasing the latest trends. It's about using your platform for something greater. The sales? They're simply the byproduct, the means to allow you to keep sharing your message with the world. When you create a social media account, you're accepting an invitation to start a conversation with anyone on the internet who comes across your profile or posts. That's powerful. And it's not a one-way street—the world gets to talk back to you too. You're not just posting; you're creating a dialogue that can reach thousands, even millions.

Think about the weight of that for a moment. You're not just shouting into the void; you're shaping perspectives, influencing decisions, and, in some cases, changing lives. That's some heavy stuff, and that's why it's so crucial to have your mental health in check. If you're not in a strong, positive mental space, that dialogue can quickly turn toxic. It's your job to ensure that you're using this platform for good, creating a positive experience not only for yourself but for the community that you're building.

Now, let's talk about sales. Yes, sales are important. They allow you to keep doing what you do, to continue showing up for your audience. But here's a hard truth: you can't lead with the sale. People can smell a sales pitch from miles away, and in today's world, we are bombarded with advertising everywhere we look. From billboards to Instagram ads, our brains are wired to tune out anything that feels like we're being sold to. So if you're simply a walking advertisement, you're going to get ignored. The real secret? Don't focus on selling. Focus on *giving*.

And no, I don't mean doing giveaways or handing out free products. Giving can be as simple as making someone smile, teaching them something new, or empowering them to take action. When you consistently give value—whether it's a helpful tip, a word of encouragement, or just a little slice of joy—you build a relationship. That relationship is the foundation of trust. And guess what trust leads to? Sales. But here's the thing: when the sale comes from a place of trust, it feels natural. It feels right, both for you and for your audience. They're not buying because you're pushing something on them. They're buying because they believe in you and the value you offer.

Consistency is key here. You can't just drop in once, provide a little value, and disappear. You need to be there, consistently showing up with new, fresh content that keeps your audience excited. They should know that when they come back to your page, they'll find something that sparks their interest, something that adds value to their life. That's how trust is built—through reliability, authenticity, and genuine connection.

What people often overlook is that personal development and being an influencer are deeply intertwined. Yes, you can experience personal growth without a social media presence, but if you're looking to build a powerful social media brand, personal development is *non-negotiable.* Why? Because growth starts with you. It's your personal evolution that makes you relatable. It's what allows you to connect with your audience on a deeper level. If you're not growing, how can you expect to inspire others to grow?

Personal growth equips you with the tools to empathize with your audience, to understand where they're coming from and to provide them with value that resonates. It's not just about having the strength to withstand criticism or negativity—it's about understanding that every person in your audience is on their own journey, and being able to support them in their growth. But here's the kicker: to help them grow, you need to be willing to grow *first*. And growth isn't always comfortable. It often means failing. But here's the secret: failure is your friend. It's your greatest teacher.

We're going to talk about failure a lot in this book because, in my experience, it's the people who are most afraid of failing that never make it to the finish line. Success, in its truest form, is found on the other side of fear and failure. You've probably heard that before, but it's worth repeating because it's so true. The most successful influencers, the ones you admire, didn't get there by playing it safe. They got there by trying, failing, and learning. And they kept going, even when it was hard.

So, here's my invitation to you: let's link arms and dive into this journey together. We're going to talk about the easy stuff, and the hard stuff, too. But the good news? You're not alone in this. I'm right here with you, every step of the way. We're all figuring this out together, and there's so much strength in that. So, take a deep breath. We're going to embrace failure, take massive action, and grow in ways you never imagined. Together, we're going to slay this social media game—are you ready?

Sparkle 1 Growth Task: Make the Commitment

Before moving forward in this book, take a moment to make a commitment to yourself. The commitment is simple but powerful:

Step 1: Write It Down
Grab a notebook, open your notes app, or even jot it down on a sticky note and say:

"I commit to showing up for myself and my social media journey. I will take consistent action, even when it's challenging, because I believe in my growth."

Step 2: Keep It Visible
Place this commitment somewhere you'll see it often—on your desk, phone background, or even as a note on your mirror. This will serve as a reminder every day to take action, no matter how big or small.

Step 3: Take the First Step
Whether it's posting something, brainstorming ideas, or simply getting organized—take one small action today that aligns with your goal of showing up consistently. This is your first step in a long but rewarding journey.

Sparkle 2: Defining Your "Why" – The Core of Authentic Influence

Let's start with a big, introspective question that might make you pause: **Who are you, really?** It's more than just what you do or what you present to the world. It's the essence of who you are, your core values, your passions, and even your quirks. The more deeply you can connect with and understand this part of yourself, the more powerfully and authentically you can show up on social media. Authenticity isn't just a buzzword—it's the foundation of everything. Without it, consistency becomes a struggle, content feels hollow, and your audience senses that disconnection.

You might feel pressure to present a perfect, polished version of yourself online. And yes, there's value in a refined image, but it must still reflect who you are at your core. I learned this the hard way. I've been working with network marketing companies for years, where duplication is the rule. The idea is to follow the leader, copy their steps, even down to their style, and then train your team to duplicate you. It's meant to build security, create consistency, and replicate success. And, for a while, it works. But after some time, I realized something important: the real magic wasn't in copying, but in showing up authentically. True connection comes when we embrace our unique qualities and help others do the same, rather than simply being carbon copies of one another.

Polishing your image doesn't mean putting on a façade that isn't aligned with who you truly are—that's exhausting and unsustainable. Authenticity gives you the freedom to show up in a way that feels sustainable and enjoyable, and that allows the energy to keep going. Social media gives you the space to express the many layers of your personality, even the edges that may feel rough. In fact, those edges are often what attract people to you because they feel real, relatable, and human. And when you step into that authentic space, you create connections and opportunities that are beyond what a mere copy-and-paste approach can offer.

We live in a world where trends come and go in a flash. It's tempting to chase what's working for others. Maybe you've caught yourself mimicking someone else's content or style, thinking, "If it works for them, it'll work for me." But here's the thing: trying to be someone else won't lead to long-term success. People crave originality, and what works for one person might fall flat for someone else. It's not about copying others but about figuring out what makes *you* unique and leaning into that.

Take a step back and think about how different creators succeed in their own lanes. For example, my daughter loves pop music, and two of her favorites are Ariana Grande and Meghan Trainor. They're both incredibly talented, but they're also incredibly different. Ariana's voice is powerful, her style is glamorous, and her music often has a moody, sensual vibe. On the other hand, Meghan has a more playful, retro sound and a body-positive, fun-loving energy. Both artists have huge followings and successful careers, yet they aren't competing to be the same. Instead, they thrive by staying true to themselves, attracting different audiences who resonate with their individual strengths and style. So, the next time you find yourself comparing yourself to others, ask yourself: "Am I trying to be Ariana Grande when I'm really more like Meghan Trainor?" The world needs both, and the same applies to you.

Once you understand that your "why" is rooted in who *you* are, not who others expect you to be, you can start focusing on the unique strengths that naturally shine through. These qualities are often the ones that draw people to you in the first place. Maybe you have an upbeat, joyful energy, a gift for storytelling, or an eye for beautiful aesthetics. When people told me my voice was too energetic or even "annoying," I began to second-guess one of my natural qualities that makes me *me.* For a while, I tried to tone it down, speaking more calmly and quietly, but I quickly noticed my views and engagement slipping. I had lost something essential—my own authentic spark! Embracing what makes you unique, rather than hiding it, is what will help you build genuine connections with your audience. Your quirks, personality, and energy bring a flavor that no one else can replicate, and that's exactly what will help you stand out.

Try to avoid focusing on your perceived flaws or dialing down what makes you different because of someone else's criticism. It's easy to feel like our imperfections hold us back, but it's often the opposite—they help others relate to us. Perhaps you've overcome struggles with self-doubt, or you've wrestled with criticism that shook your confidence, just as I did. Sharing your journey and the lessons you've learned from these challenges can be incredibly empowering for your audience. When we show up as our real, imperfect selves, we invite others to feel comfortable doing the same. Don't underestimate how much your story and true personality can inspire others to feel comfortable in their own skin. You don't need to be anyone but *you* to make an impact. Your authenticity and vulnerability might just be the key that connects you to someone who needs to see that they can show up as themselves too.

Here's a challenge: make a list of the struggles you've overcome in your life. You might be surprised by how much you've grown and how much knowledge you've gained without even realizing it. Those challenges were likely blessings in disguise, shaping who you are today. By sharing these parts of your journey, you provide value beyond what's trendy or visually appealing. You're giving your audience something real, something that touches hearts and can even change lives. And that's where true influence comes from—not from perfection, but from authenticity, empathy, and connection.

Don't underestimate the impact of something as simple as a smile. A smile can light up a room, and on social media, it can light up a feed. Your energy is contagious, whether it's positive or negative. So, if you show up with genuine positivity, even in small moments, you create an atmosphere that people want to be a part of. You attract others who are drawn to that same vibe. You don't have to be a "cheese ball," but you also don't have to hold back. Stop dimming your light. Let it shine! The world needs your unique energy, and there's no reason to hide it.

Let's rethink branding. Many people get stuck on the idea that branding is a logo, color scheme, or even the products they offer. While these elements are part of a brand, true branding runs far deeper—it's an experience, a feeling. Branding is the emotional response your presence inspires in others. When people encounter your content, how does it make them feel? Are they inspired to reflect on their own journey?

Do they feel understood, entertained, or motivated?
This emotional connection is the heart of your brand,
and it's built on who you genuinely are. To create this
connection, start by exploring what evokes those
feelings in you.

Think about what brings you joy. What activities,
people, or moments spark that pure, childlike
happiness? Perhaps it's the freedom of dancing around
your kitchen while making dinner, or the calm that
fills you after a morning meditation. These sources of
joy aren't just personal—they are unique expressions
of who you are and can be powerful parts of your
brand. When you connect with these parts of yourself,
it naturally comes through in your content. And your
audience, drawn to this authenticity, feels the same
energy. Joy isn't a strategy; it's a presence. By sharing
what truly fulfills you, you invite others to share in
that fulfillment, making your brand magnetic in a way
that's impossible to replicate.

Equally important are your values, the beliefs that
drive your choices and shape the way you show up
online. These are the principles that make you proud
and grounded. For instance, while some people may
build their brand through direct sales tactics, you
might choose a different path—one rooted in
connection, authenticity, and creating value through
attraction. Instead of pushing products, you're sharing
parts of yourself, your journey, and insights that

resonate. People are drawn in, not because you've reached out to them but because they see themselves reflected in your story. They feel aligned with your values—kindness, creativity, perseverance, or authenticity—and that alignment fosters trust. Although it may feel slower than more aggressive methods, this approach is built to last. Your values don't just guide your content; they create a brand that is authentic, sustainable, and deeply meaningful.

When you're clear on what brings you joy and what you stand for, you can align your online identity with your real-life identity. This alignment is what makes your presence feel natural and effortless, and it's what will help you build a strong, lasting connection with your audience. Your purpose as an influencer isn't just to gain followers or likes—it's to create a space where people feel understood, inspired, and uplifted. When you can do that, your influence becomes far more meaningful than any trend or viral post.

So, as you continue your journey as an influencer, don't just focus on the surface-level aspects of your brand. Go deeper. Define your "why." Understand who you are, what brings you joy, and what values you want to share with the world. That's the foundation of authentic influence, and it's what will sustain you in this ever-changing digital landscape.

Sparkle 2 Growth Tasks: Defining Your "Why"

1. Reflect on Your Core Values: Take 10-15 minutes to write down 3-5 values that are most important to you. These could be kindness, creativity, authenticity, or anything else that feels true to who you are. Think about how you can integrate these values into your content.

2. Identify Your Strengths: Write a list of your strengths—skills, talents, or qualities that make you unique. This could be anything from storytelling to making people laugh, to being a great listener. How can you showcase these strengths in your social media content?

3. Celebrate Your Flaws: Make a list of a few "flaws" or challenges you've overcome that have shaped who you are today. Consider how sharing these stories can help others relate to you and find comfort in their own struggles.

4. Create a Joy List: What brings you that childlike sense of joy? Write down 5-10 things that make you feel genuinely happy. Consider how you can incorporate these joyful moments into your content to bring more positivity and authenticity to your brand.

5. Define Your Audience's Experience: Think about the feeling you want your audience to have when they interact with your content. What vibe are you creating? Is it fun, comforting, inspiring? Write down three words that describe the emotional experience you want to cultivate, and brainstorm ways to infuse your content with those feelings.

6. Write a Mission Statement: Based on your reflections, write a short mission statement (1-2 sentences) that expresses your "why" and the value you want to bring to your audience. This will help you stay aligned as you create content moving forward.

Sparkle 3: Building Confidence – Being Unapologetically You

There will come a time, in fact many times, okay, let's be real—most or all of the time—when you'll doubt yourself being on camera and sharing your message with the world. You'll second-guess if people think you look silly, wonder if it's dumb that you're pursuing this whole social media thing, and start imagining that the whole world is talking about you. But here's the truth: most people aren't paying as much attention as you think. In fact, it might surprise you to know—people are so caught up in their own lives that they probably won't even notice that awkward blink or the moment you stumbled over a word.

In today's world, it's normal for everyone and their dogs—literally, we've all seen those cute puppy pages!—to be on social media. Yes, people will stop and watch your videos. Yes, they may comment or like them. But here's the reality check: nobody looks at your content as closely as you do. You are your harshest critic. When someone sees your video, they're spending 30–60 seconds out of their 86,400 seconds in a day. That's it. And, in most cases, whatever they saw will fade from their memory within minutes. It's easy to think they're scrutinizing every detail, but they aren't. What will stick with them longer, however, is the feeling you leave them with—how your message resonates with them emotionally, or how relatable you are.

That's what matters: the connection, the authenticity, the repetition of those moments when they felt heard or inspired by you. As we discussed in the last chapter when we touched on branding, those emotional connections are what ultimately create something great.

Feeling Like a Fake – Imposter Syndrome at Work

So, if you're being yourself, why does it sometimes feel like you're faking it? Why do you feel like everyone is silently judging you? This is imposter syndrome creeping in, and it's something most people face, especially when putting themselves out there publicly. You may also have a healthy dose of self-doubt—it's completely normal. When you first start getting on camera, it doesn't feel natural for anyone, no matter how authentic you aim to be. It's new, it's vulnerable, and you're literally putting yourself out there for the world to see. But this doesn't make you fake—it simply means you're facing a new, very human fear.

This fear, though intimidating, is also an incredible opportunity for growth. Overcoming it can be truly transformative, and I've seen it happen time and again—both in my own life and in the lives of others. Getting on camera is, at its core, an internal challenge.

The physical action is simple: you press record, you speak, you share. But it's what happens inside that makes this feel like a monumental feat. It's not just about how others see you; it's about how you see yourself.

We're simply not used to seeing ourselves talk, express, and exist outside a mirror. This perspective brings a heightened level of self-awareness that can feel unfamiliar or even uncomfortable. We hear our voice differently than we do in our head, and we see our facial expressions from an angle usually reserved for others. Many people go through life without being hyper-aware of these aspects of themselves, and suddenly, getting on camera brings it all into focus. You're given a front-row seat to your own mannerisms, quirks, and voice, which can feel both strange and eye-opening.

Yet facing this discomfort and embracing it is a powerful act. As you lean into this self-awareness, you begin to expand your comfort zone. The journey may feel awkward at first, but once you conquer this vulnerability, you'll find yourself facing other fears with newfound courage. Your confidence will bloom, and before you know it, you'll be tackling challenges and taking risks you never thought you would—all because you dared to be seen on camera.

Remember, being on camera isn't about vanity or ego. You're not putting on a show or trying to be someone you're not. You're simply showing up as your authentic self because you have something valuable to share with the world. Don't let anyone's opinion convince you otherwise. Each time you step in front of the camera, you're not just sharing a message—you're owning your presence, embracing your true self, and offering something meaningful to those who need it.

The Power of Letting Go of Opinions

One of my favorite quotes says something along the lines of "the opinions of other people are none of my business." The first time I heard this, I had to sit with it for a while. It felt uncomfortable at first—I thought, 'of course it's my business, it's about me!' But the more I thought about it, the more freeing it became. Why should I allow someone else's opinion, someone who doesn't know my journey, to dictate whether I share my message or not? Letting a negative comment stop me would mean I'm letting one voice prevent me from possibly helping countless others who need to hear what I have to say. Their negative opinion doesn't get to take that opportunity from me, and they certainly don't get to take that information from those that need it, not on my watch. & now, this mindset shift now can become the drive and motivation to do it anyway. Thank you a-hole. Lol.

It's a mindset shift that takes time, but once you embrace it, it's empowering. Remember, the opinions of others are often momentary, based on their own insecurities or biases. Don't let them stop you from doing something that could positively impact someone's life.

There's No Magic Formula

Here's the truth I wish I could sugarcoat for you: there's no magical formula for instantly building confidence on camera. I wish I could give you a step-by-step guide that would make it easy, but the reality is, you just have to rip the bandaid off and do it. Of course, there are ways to ease yourself in, to make it feel less daunting, but the more you avoid it, the more time you give yourself to overthink and talk yourself out of it too. Confidence doesn't come from avoiding fear—it comes from confronting it. So, I'm going to give you some tips to take some baby steps if you really, really need them. But honestly, I think anything that isn't just doing the dang thing is an avoidance behavior. But baby steps are still better than no steps. Standing still is always the only way to fail, so in lieu of some people holding completely still I'll give you these avoidance tips - I mean baby steps... whatever you want to call them.

Easing Into Video Content: Practical Tips

Start small. If going live on camera feels overwhelming, begin with selfies. Selfies offer a controlled environment—you can take a hundred shots, choose the perfect one, write a caption, and boom—you've posted. It's a safe way to start engaging with your audience visually without diving into the deep end of video content just yet.

Here are a few tips for great selfies that will help you build confidence and connect with your audience:

1. **Find Your Best Lighting**: Natural light is your best friend for selfies. Position yourself near a window or in soft outdoor light. This adds warmth to your features and avoids harsh shadows. If natural light isn't available, a ring light can help create a similar effect indoors.
2. **Experiment with Angles**: Don't be afraid to try different angles! Holding the camera slightly above eye level is generally flattering, but play around to find the angle that feels most "you." Tilting your head or using a slight side angle can add interest and dimension to the shot.
3. **Focus on Your Expression**: A genuine smile or subtle expression can convey your personality better than a forced pose. Imagine talking to a friend, or think of something that genuinely

makes you happy—this can bring a natural, authentic look to your selfie.

4. **Mind Your Background**: Clean, uncluttered backgrounds let you shine in the frame. Experiment with different backgrounds that feel on-brand or that showcase a part of your personality, like your workspace, favorite coffee spot, or a colorful wall.

5. **Use Self-Timer or Burst Mode**: If holding the camera feels awkward, try setting up your phone on a stable surface and using the self-timer. Burst mode is also great—it captures several frames at once, so you have more options to choose from. Another idea I use often is to take a video, and then pull still images from the video.

6. **Edit, But Don't Overdo It**: Filters and basic edits can enhance your selfie, but subtle adjustments can keep it feeling authentic. Adjust brightness, contrast, and maybe add a little warmth, but avoid heavy filters that drastically change your appearance.

While selfies are great and an important part of your content plan, video content is incredibly powerful. Video helps your audience connect with you on a much deeper level, allowing them to see your expressions, hear your voice, and really get a sense of your personality. To start, try pre-recording short clips. The beauty of pre-recorded videos is that you can take as many takes as you need until you feel comfortable. You're in control, which makes it an ideal way to practice.

If you're new to short-form video, here are some tips to help you get started:

1. **Begin with Quick Introductions:** Start with simple, brief videos where you introduce yourself, share a fun fact, or talk about your day. Short introductions give your audience a feel for who you are without requiring complex editing or long-winded scripts.
2. **Plan Your Content Ahead:** Write down a few bullet points to guide you before you start filming. This doesn't have to be a strict script but rather a loose guide to keep you on track. Knowing what you want to say will help you feel more confident and reduce the number of takes needed.
3. **Experiment with Camera Placement:** Place your camera or phone at eye level for a more natural look. Stabilize it with a tripod or prop it up on a steady surface to avoid shaky footage, which can be distracting. Filming from a comfortable, steady angle helps you focus on your delivery.
4. **Keep it Short and Sweet:** Short-form videos thrive across platforms like Instagram Reels,

TikTok, and YouTube Shorts. Aim for 15 to 30 seconds to start. This short duration keeps it manageable, reduces pressure, and helps you learn how to condense your message.

5. **Get Creative with Edits**: Use built-in platform tools to add text, music, or transitions to make your videos more engaging. If you're camera-shy, start with videos that feature captions or text overlays, letting you narrate without necessarily being in every frame.

6. **Practice Facial Expressions and Tone**: Practice in front of a mirror or during your recordings to see how your expressions and voice come across. Speak a little slower than usual and emphasize key words. A warm smile and enthusiastic tone can make a big difference in connecting with your viewers.

Once you feel ready, Instagram even has a *practice mode* for going live, which allows you to simulate the experience without anyone actually watching. It's a fantastic tool to get comfortable with the feeling of going live, and who knows—by the end of it, you might feel confident enough to post it anyway, which Instagram also offers as an option!

The Power of Going Live

But here's my bold recommendation: go live. Like, the real, talk to your audience while they watch kind of live. Yes, it's scary. Yes, it feels like jumping off a cliff. But here's the thing—there's something incredibly liberating about facing your fear head-on. When you go live, tell your audience that you're nervous. Be open about it. Share what you're doing and why it's meaningful to you. People love authenticity, and being vulnerable is the quickest way to build that genuine connection.

I still remember my first live video. My face was beet-red, my hands were shaking, and I'm pretty sure my armpits were a full-blown waterworks show. But guess what? It was worth it! Each time I went live after that, it got easier, and now it feels natural. I realized something important—it's actually easier to talk to a camera than to stand in front of a room full of people. Going live helped me overcome not just my fear of the camera, but it also eased my social anxiety in other areas of my life.

Comparing Yourself to Others

Lastly, remember to go easy on yourself and avoid falling into the comparison trap. Social media may be packed with people who seem like they have it all together—glossy images, polished videos, effortless captions. But keep in mind, behind every successful influencer is a journey of trial, error, growth, and resilience. Even those who seem most confident and collected started exactly where you are: at the very beginning, with shaky first attempts, plenty of self-doubt, and a dream.

If it helps, give yourself permission to step back from scrolling through others' content altogether, especially at the start. Focus on creating rather than consuming. When we're constantly watching others, it's easy to feel like we don't measure up or that our content somehow lacks. But real growth and confidence come from the doing—from rolling up your sleeves and putting in the work. Your voice, your style, and your unique spark can only come alive when you stop trying to mimic others and start crafting something that's authentically you.

So, I dare you—get brave and bold. Rip off the bandaid, count to three, and just do it. Feel the energy in your body, take a deep breath, and trust yourself. Jump up and down if it helps, get your blood pumping, and remember that every tiny step you take is a building block in your journey. You've got this—no one can bring what you bring to the table, and I know you have something incredible to share.

Even if you don't feel like a total badass just yet, let me remind you that you are. Every day you show up, you're paving the way toward a stronger, more confident you. So, believe in yourself, even if it's just for a few seconds. Take the leap because I believe in you wholeheartedly, and I know you have what it takes to shine.

Sparkle 3 Growth Tasks: Building Confidence – Being Unapologetically You

1. **Selfie Challenge:** Start by taking 5 selfies over the next week and posting them with a caption that reflects your personality. Focus on showing your authentic self, whether it's sharing a thought, an emotion, or a funny moment from your day. Let go of perfectionism and remember, this is about practice, not perfection.

2. **Short-Form Video Practice:** Create a short 15–30 second video introducing yourself and your social media purpose. This can be pre-recorded, so take as many tries as you need. Don't overthink it—just let your personality shine. Share the video on your preferred platform.

3. **Live Video Simulation:** If you're feeling nervous about going live, try using Instagram's "practice mode" this week. Get used to the feeling of talking on camera without the pressure of an audience. Once you've finished, reflect on how it felt, and decide if you want to share the recording publicly.

4. **Face Your Fear – Go Live:** Commit to going live for the first time! Choose a date and time, and go live for at least 3 minutes. Be open about your nerves and share why you're stepping out

of your comfort zone. Even if you only have one person watching, it's a win! This is a huge step, so celebrate it.

5. **Positive Affirmations:** Write down three positive affirmations to tell yourself before recording or going live. For example: "I have something valuable to share," "I am proud of showing up authentically," or "I am improving with every video." Say these aloud before each filming session to help boost your confidence.

6. **Compare Mindfully:** Identify three influencers or creators you admire and write down what you love about their content. Then, list three unique qualities you bring to the table that set you apart. This will help you focus on your strengths instead of falling into the comparison trap.

7. **Reflect and Adjust:** After completing each action task, write down what worked, what didn't, and how you felt. Were there moments when your confidence spiked? Did you notice any mental shifts? Adjust your approach as needed, but most importantly, keep going!

Sparkle 4: Mental Health in the Digital Space

I've been sharing on social media for over a decade, and during that time, I've learned so much about the power of the digital world. However, despite all of its potential for good, I still do not allow my three teenagers to have phones—especially not social media accounts. Why? Because while social media can be a powerful tool, it can also expose developing brains to things they are not emotionally or mentally equipped to handle. I can't imagine how I would have navigated the emotional rollercoaster of my teenage years if social media had been around. Being a teenager is hard enough without the constant comparison, exposure to perfection, and relentless pressure to be seen or heard that social media often brings. It amplifies every insecurity, every awkward moment, and every intense feeling—sometimes in harmful ways.

Let me start off this chapter with an essential warning: if you're looking to grow on social media, make sure you're in a good mental space before diving in. You might be eager to start your journey or expand your influence, but social media can amplify underlying emotional challenges if you're not ready. If you choose to proceed despite this caution, it's important to equip yourself with the right coping tools to manage your mental health—these are tools we all need, whether we're new to the platform or experienced professionals.

This chapter isn't the fun, glamorous part of social media growth—quite the opposite. It's the uncomfortable, sometimes messy side of things. Social media, as I've already expressed in earlier chapters, has tremendous potential. It's an incredible space for connection, education, inspiration, and growth. I love it for those reasons. But where there's yin, there's yang. The digital space also has a dark side, filled with traps that can lead to harmful outcomes if not approached with care. Anxiety, depression, feelings of inadequacy, social comparison, burnout, addiction—all of these are very real issues that social media can intensify.

For many of us, the addictive nature of social media isn't something we notice until we're deep in it. The immediate gratification of likes, shares, and comments becomes a source of validation, and before we know it, we're obsessing over the metrics. We chase growth like it's the only thing that matters.

But here's the thing: growth doesn't happen overnight. Building an influence, creating a business, or making an impact takes time. Trying to force it to happen quickly only leads to burnout. That's why patience, mindfulness, and intentional mental health practices are not just beneficial—they are essential.

It's easy to get so wrapped up in the numbers that you lose sight of *why* you started in the first place. When your focus shifts entirely to metrics—how many likes, views, or followers you have—you risk disconnecting from your deeper purpose. And it's your purpose that fuels your passion and drive.

Without that connection to your "why," the work starts to feel hollow. The pressure to constantly grow can take the joy out of creating, leading to frustration, exhaustion, and eventually burnout. Ironically, when burnout hits, it doesn't just harm your mental health—it halts your growth altogether. Your audience can sense when your energy is forced or inauthentic. Authenticity and enthusiasm are what draw people in, and when those are missing, it becomes harder to maintain meaningful connections with your community.

To avoid falling into this trap, it's crucial to realign with your purpose regularly. Take time to reflect on the reason you began your journey. What impact do you want to make? Who do you want to help or inspire? These questions can serve as your anchor when the pull of metrics becomes too strong.

Instead of obsessing over the numbers, shift your focus to what you can control—creating content that resonates, fostering genuine connections, and taking care of your mental health. Remember that growth isn't just about quantity; it's about quality. When you nurture your purpose, you'll find that growth happens naturally over time—and in a way that feels sustainable and fulfilling.

By prioritizing your mental health and staying connected to your purpose, you can create a social media presence that's not only impactful but also a true reflection of your values and passion.

One of the key lessons I've learned is the importance of establishing strong boundaries between your online persona and your private life. It's easy to feel like you owe your followers access to every part of your world, but that's not true. Boundaries aren't about being fake or inauthentic—they're about protecting your well-being. Sharing your life doesn't mean putting everything on display. It's about choosing what's meaningful and healthy to share while keeping other aspects private and sacred. You can still be authentic while drawing those lines.

Having boundaries also means knowing when to step away from the screen. In the hyper-connected world of social media, it's easy to blur the lines between your work life and your personal life. But here's the truth: to truly be present in your life, you need to disconnect. When you're having dinner with your family, for example, be present at the table. That means no phone, no notifications—just time with your loved ones. And at night, let your body rest by putting your phone down. Blue light from screens disrupts your sleep patterns, and when you're constantly checking social media before bed, you're not giving yourself the real, restorative rest you need.

Then there's the issue of mindless scrolling, something we're all guilty of at times. The problem with scrolling isn't just the time it eats up—it's the passive consumption of other people's content. As an influencer, your goal should be to create more than you consume. If you find yourself falling into the scroll trap, set limits. Take a walk, go outside, do something active. The goal is to stay mindful of how much time you're spending taking in versus creating. Remember, you are here to impact and influence others, not to be swept away by the wave of content coming at you.

For me, a game-changer has been treating social media like a real job. Whether you're all-in, working part-time, or pursuing social media as a passion project, the structure is essential if you want to thrive and feel balanced. This can be especially challenging when your "office" is also your home. Even if you don't have a dedicated workspace, consider creating a small area or a "work zone" that you reserve just for content creation or planning sessions. Try setting up in a corner with a specific chair, a small desk organizer, or even a favorite mug to help signal to your brain that you're in work mode. When you step away from this spot, it becomes easier to leave the work mindset behind and be fully present with family or unwind.

Time-blocking has been one of the best tools for staying focused and avoiding burnout. I break my day into dedicated chunks for content creation, family time, work, exercise, and self-care. Each block has a purpose, and I treat every block with the respect it deserves. A quick "reset" ritual between blocks can help clear your head and reset your focus: take a deep breath, stretch, or step outside for a moment before diving into the next part of your day. When you approach each time block as a fresh start, you're giving yourself permission to be fully present, whether you're planning a reel, sitting down for family dinner, or working out.

Creating content isn't just about recording and posting—it's about the full process, from brainstorming and scripting to editing and polishing. Time-blocking lets you go deep into each part of the process without feeling rushed. When you've clearly set boundaries around your work time and have a plan for each block, it becomes much easier to resist distractions and be present during your personal time. You can dive fully into family life, self-care, or relaxation, knowing you have dedicated time to come back to your work, refreshed and recharged.

Self-care and mental health go hand in hand. Without them, you won't have the energy or emotional resilience to continue on your journey. It's important to understand what fills your cup and makes you feel recharged. Maybe it's reading a book, engaging in a creative hobby, playing a game with your kids, or going on a nature walk. The key is knowing when to step back and give yourself that time. You are the center of everything you are creating, so nurturing yourself needs to be a priority.

Becoming a mom added a whole new layer to my understanding. In my children's early years, my days were so filled with meeting others' needs and learning to survive that I nearly forgot about the little joys I used to savor, like enjoying a sunset in silence, heading into the forest on a trail run, or diving into a book without distractions. These simple pleasures—often easily cast aside in the rush of motherhood and daily demands—were, in hindsight, a huge part of my own resilience and happiness.

If you're in that same place, start by asking yourself: What little moments used to make me feel most at ease? Think back to a time before the responsibilities piled up. Did you love savoring a cup of coffee in the quiet of the morning? Did you get lost in journaling, art, music, or cooking? Maybe you had a favorite spot in town to wander or a cozy nook to curl up with a good book.

Sometimes, old photo albums or journals can be powerful reminders. Try flipping through pictures of those times or jotting down a list of favorite memories.

Another idea is to set aside just a few minutes each week to explore one small joy you haven't experienced in a while. It doesn't have to be extravagant—just something that reconnects you to who you were before life got so full. A simple one that I re-visited was doing crossword puzzles. It was something I could pick up easily for a 5 minute break and come back to again later, and it was something I enjoyed - just for me. I had a therapist once tell me that these small "just for you" things are most beneficial if it doesn't benefit anyone else in any way when you do them. It's all about remembering how important you are too, and making *your* happiness a priority - so you can then, in turn, be there in a positive way for others.

Reclaiming these moments, even if only in small, intentional ways, is part of staying grounded. They remind us we're more than our to-do lists, and they help us nurture the creative, passionate, unique parts of ourselves. Little by little, these moments of joy and self-reflection can breathe life back into the daily grind, keeping you whole and reminding you that your own happiness is worth the time.

At the end of the day, mental health is not just something to think about occasionally—it should be woven into the very fabric of your social media strategy nearly every day. Take the time to pause, reflect, and build in space to care for yourself. Social media is a powerful tool, but it should never come at the expense of your well-being. Your influence and impact only grow stronger when you're grounded, centered, and in a healthy headspace.

Sparkle 4 Growth Tasks: Prioritizing Mental Health in Your Social Media Journey

1. **Create a Social Media Time Audit**
    Track the amount of time you spend on social media for one week. Note how much time you dedicate to creating content versus consuming it. At the end of the week, reflect on whether the balance feels right and identify areas where you can reduce passive scrolling or consumption.

2. **Set Time Blocks for Social Media Engagement**
    Pick specific times each day or week to engage with social media. During these blocks, focus solely on content creation, responding to followers, or engaging with your audience. Outside of those blocks, commit to staying off your phone or away from social media to create clear work-life boundaries.

3. **Develop a Pre-Bedtime Digital Detox Routine**
    Establish a nightly routine where you disconnect from your phone and social media at least one hour before bed. Use this time to wind down with activities that relax you, such as reading, journaling, or meditating. This will improve your sleep and give your mind the rest it needs.

4. **Designate Screen-Free Zones and Times**
    Choose certain areas in your home (like the

dining table or bedroom) or specific times of the day (such as family dinners or morning routines) to be screen-free. Make it a habit to be fully present during these moments, and encourage others in your household to do the same.

5. **Create a Self-Care Menu**
    Make a list of activities that recharge you and boost your mental well-being. These could be as simple as going for a walk, practicing yoga, or painting. Commit to incorporating at least one of these activities into your week to help you step away from the screen and reconnect with yourself.

6. **Set Boundaries with Your Audience**
    Write down three specific boundaries you will set regarding what you share on social media. These might include protecting your personal life, limiting how often you respond to comments, or defining what types of personal information you won't share. Stick to these boundaries to protect your mental health.

7. **Reflect on Your "Why"**
    Take a moment to revisit why you're on social media in the first place. Write down your core reasons for showing up online and how they align with your long-term goals. Use this reflection as a reminder to stay grounded in

your purpose when challenges or pressures arise.

8. **Unfollow or Mute Accounts That Don't Serve You**

   Go through your social media feeds and remove any accounts that make you feel inadequate, anxious, or overly negative. Instead, fill your feed with positive, inspiring, and uplifting content that aligns with your personal growth journey.

Sparkle 5: Social Media Strategy – Growing with Intention

If you're a planner at heart, you're going to love this chapter. If not, bear with me - because planning is a major game changer. Here, we'll dive into the layout for your social media presence, giving you the tools to plan and lay down the ground rules for the what, when, how, and why of everything you do online. Social media without strategy is like building a house without a blueprint—it's chaotic, inconsistent, and unlikely to withstand the test of time. But with a well-crafted plan, you'll be able to build a solid foundation for long-term success, grounded in intention and purpose.

By now, you've already been crafting your "why," but as we move forward, you'll notice that your why is often quite different from your specific goals. Your why gives you a sense of purpose—it's your motivation. But your goals? Those are the measurable targets you set to track your progress. Your goal might be to drive more sales, which means you'll want to focus on funneling traffic to your website or online store. Maybe your goal is to spread a message, in which case your focus will be on engagement and interaction—sparking conversations and encouraging dialogue. Perhaps you want to build your follower count (not always my favorite goal, but for some, it's essential). Or maybe you're still in the process of figuring out your goals altogether, and that's perfectly fine too.

The key is to align your goals *with* your why. When these two elements come together, they act like a compass for your social media strategy. Once you have clarity on your why and your goals, you can begin crafting a strategy designed to fit your desired outcome.

While I'd love to give you all the platform-specific strategies right here in this chapter, the reality is that social media changes so rapidly that by the time you're reading this, some of those tactics may already be outdated. So rather than focus too much on technical specifics, I want to teach you timeless strategies. And hey—if you want up-to-date, platform-specific tips for the moment you're reading this, especially for Instagram (which is my specialty), I'd be happy to chat! You can always book a one-on-one session with me through my Instagram page @sparkleandgrow, where we can dive into the details together for your specific needs.

But let's keep things general for now. No matter the platform, your strategy will likely include a combination of photos, graphics, stories, short-form videos (like Instagram Reels or TikToks), and long-form videos (such as YouTube). Each format serves different audiences and purposes. For example, currently on Instagram, photos tend to reach your existing followers, while Reels are more likely to attract new viewers who don't already follow you. Keeping up with platform updates is important, but don't let yourself get bogged down in obsessing over every minor change. Social media is a constantly evolving landscape. The best thing you can do is stay true to your brand, your purpose, and your audience. The rest will follow.

One strategy that can help you maintain focus while keeping things fresh is to work with content "pillars" or "buckets." These terms are used interchangeably, but they both refer to the core themes or categories your social media will revolve around. When you're building a personal brand, your niche might not be as narrowly defined as someone selling a product, but that's okay—because *you* are the niche. However, even personal brands need structure, which is where these pillars come in.

Think of your pillars as the different topics or areas of your life that you want to share with your audience. For someone with a beauty business, for instance, pillars might look like this: makeup looks, makeup tutorials, skincare tips, fashion, and hair tutorials. If you're running a fitness brand, your pillars might focus on different aspects of your program: leg day, arm workouts, core exercises, nutrition tips, and motivational content.

For personal brands, your pillars might be more diverse and lifestyle-oriented. Let's say you're a personal influencer who loves food and fashion. Your pillars could be things like: food diary, daily routines, my dog, favorite restaurants, and outfit of the day. Notice how each category flows naturally from your life—these are the things that make you *you*. They should feel organic and authentic to share. That way, it's not forced or contrived; it's a reflection of who you truly are.

The purpose of having these pillars is to ensure that your content stays interesting and varied while remaining cohesive. It's easy to fall into the trap of being too random, especially when you have so many interests. But if your content lacks a clear focus, it becomes difficult for your audience to understand what you're about. By narrowing it down to 3-5 key pillars, you can provide value in each area while still maintaining a sense of consistency. Think of your pillars as the framework that holds your brand together.

Having a few core pillars also makes it easier to use data to your advantage. Analytics can be incredibly valuable in helping you understand what resonates with your audience. If you notice that your posts featuring your dog always get more engagement, you can start incorporating your dog into more content. Maybe your audience loves motivational content but

isn't as interested in your food diary. The beauty of
pillars is that they give you the flexibility to test
different types of content while staying true to your
brand.

But here's the key—don't be too quick to pivot. Social
media requires patience, and your analytics might not
give you accurate insights until you've consistently
tested something for at least 3-6 months. Sometimes,
it takes your audience a while to catch onto a new type
of content or a new direction you're taking. If you
don't give your strategy enough time to breathe, you
could miss out on valuable data. Social media is not a
sprint—it's a marathon. Growth doesn't happen
overnight, and neither does building a lasting
connection with your audience.

It's also important to remember that data can be
misleading if you're only looking at short-term trends.
One post might go viral, while another might flop, but
it doesn't necessarily mean one type of content is
inherently better than the other. You need to look at
the bigger picture. Analyze trends over time, not just
in isolated posts. Use your analytics to see what's
working, but don't let a few anomalies dictate your
entire strategy. Trends and viral posts are temporary,
and you want stable long-term growth that keeps you
afloat.

Ultimately, the best social media strategies are the ones that are grounded in both intention and flexibility. You need a plan, but you also need to be willing to adapt as things change. Social media will throw curveballs at you—algorithm changes, new features, or shifts in your audience's preferences. But when you have a strong foundation, you'll be better equipped to adjust and keep moving forward without losing sight of your goals.

One of the most misunderstood aspects of social media is the algorithm. It's easy to think of it as a puzzle to solve or a challenge to conquer, but this mindset can lead to frustration and burnout. Instead, consider the algorithm as a tool—a way platforms organize and deliver the type of content your audience wants to see. The algorithm isn't trying to hide your content or sabotage your growth; it's designed to serve the audience and not the other way around.

Here's a helpful tip: when trying to figure out what the algorithm "wants," replace the word *algorithm* with *audience*. Ask yourself, "What does my audience want?" This subtle shift in perspective can help you focus on creating meaningful, engaging content rather than obsessing over trends or hacks. After all, the algorithm isn't the one clicking 'like' or sharing your posts—your audience is.

When you understand your audience's preferences and how they align with your brand, you naturally create content that works *with* the algorithm rather than against it. This doesn't mean ignoring trends completely; it means being selective. If a trend aligns with your brand and resonates with your audience, embrace it. If it doesn't, let it go. Staying authentic to your mission and values will always win in the long run.

Remember, your job isn't to beat the algorithm; it's to connect with the people who are meant to hear your message. Prioritize quality over quantity, intention over imitation, and engagement over vanity metrics. The better you know your audience, the better you can adapt your strategy—not to game the system, but to build genuine, lasting connections.

In the end, the most powerful strategy is one that feels right for you and serves your audience. Social media may evolve, but when you focus on serving your community, you'll grow with it. Let the algorithm be your guide, not your competition.

Once you've found a rhythm in your content, growing your engagement and reach is all about small, intentional adjustments that bring your audience into a conversation. Consider each post as a chance to connect, not just to broadcast. By encouraging your followers to engage with you, you transform passive viewers into active participants. A simple question in your caption, a "fill-in-the-blank" prompt, or a relatable call-to-action can invite valuable interactions, boosting not only engagement but the depth of your community. People love to share their thoughts and experiences, so give them ways to chime in that feel natural and inviting.

Every social media platform offers features to drive connection, and taking advantage of these can strengthen your presence. Interactive tools like Instagram's Stories allow you to run polls, ask questions, or give followers a behind-the-scenes look at your world, deepening their connection to your brand. When people feel like they're getting a special glimpse or contributing to a conversation, they're more likely to engage consistently. These types of features aren't just add-ons—they're ways to involve your audience in real-time, making them feel valued and heard.

To sustain this connection, focus on sharing "saveable" content that brings practical value. Tips, insights, or inspirational posts tend to attract more saves, a powerful engagement metric that can signal to algorithms that your content is worth sharing widely. Think of it as creating a resource that your followers can return to, share, and learn from over time. Posts that resonate deeply tend to reach broader audiences naturally, further expanding your growth potential.

Remember, there's no "magic number" of times to post each week that guarantees success. It's different for everyone, and the ideal frequency depends on how much time you have to dedicate and what your goals are. Consistency matters far more than quantity, so find a routine that works for you and stick with it. If you're able to post more frequently and can maintain quality, that's fantastic—but don't feel pressured to post more at the expense of value. An engaged community responds better to meaningful content than to rushed, frequent updates, so let your schedule be one that you can sustain comfortably and effectively.

User-generated content, or UGC, is another strong tool for engagement and credibility. When you invite followers to share their experiences with your brand, they not only feel acknowledged but become advocates for your content or product. This can be as simple as encouraging your community to tag you in their posts or creating a campaign that highlights their stories. A photo challenge or feature series can create excitement around your brand while showcasing real-life connections with your audience. Not only does this generate organic engagement, but it also builds trust by showing real-world examples of your product's impact.

Building urgency can be a useful way to convert engagement into sales, especially when done sparingly and authentically. Occasional flash sales or time-sensitive offers motivate your audience to act, especially if they're already invested in your brand. However, balance is key—too many promotional posts can come across as forced, so let these moments be just one aspect of your overall content.

At the heart of all these strategies is consistency and experimentation. Show up regularly, and be open to trying new types of posts or content formats, whether it's a reel, carousel, or live Q&A session. Discovering what resonates with your audience comes from testing and being flexible. Strategy is about learning and adjusting over time, not about locking yourself into rigid patterns. By experimenting, you'll not only find what feels right for your brand but also naturally adapt to shifting audience preferences.

To keep your growth intentional, analyzing the results of your efforts is crucial. Track engagement and key metrics, and look for trends that point to what your audience truly values. Metrics like saves, shares, and comments can reveal what resonates most, helping you refine future content. Beyond engagement, consider which posts generate website clicks or product inquiries, as these insights offer a fuller picture of what drives your business goals. Social media growth is as much about understanding your audience's changing preferences as it is about content itself, so let these metrics be your guide.

Ultimately, by focusing on genuine connection and remaining adaptable, you'll craft a strategy that doesn't just bring more followers but builds a loyal community. Rather than chasing trends or algorithms, let your audience's needs guide you as you grow. The more authentic and value-driven your content, the more naturally your brand will thrive. Social media becomes less about competition and more about fostering a meaningful exchange. Stay flexible, keep listening, and evolve with the platform to build a brand that's not only successful but deeply resonant with those who follow you.

Sparkle 5 Growth Tasks: Crafting Your Social Media Strategy with Intention

1. **Define Your Goals**
   Take a moment to write down your primary social media goals. Are you looking to increase engagement, drive sales, or grow your follower count? Be specific, and ensure your goals align with your "why."

2. **Identify Your Pillars**
   List 3-5 content pillars that reflect who you are and what you want to share. Consider your passions, expertise, and what feels natural for you to post about. These will guide your content creation moving forward.

3. **Understand Your Audience**
   Replace the word *algorithm* with *audience* in your strategy mindset. Write a few sentences about what your audience truly wants from your content. What problems can you solve for them? What inspires or entertains them? Let this understanding guide your future posts.

4. **Conduct a Content Audit**
   Review your past social media posts and categorize them based on your new pillars. Identify which types of content performed well and which didn't. This will help you understand your audience's preferences and refine your approach.

5. **Create a Content Calendar**
   Plan out your content for the next month using your pillars. Schedule specific topics for each week to ensure a balanced mix of content. Focus on creating value for your audience rather than chasing trends.

6. **Experiment and Analyze**
   Choose one new type of content or format (like Reels, stories, or infographics) to try over the next month. After that time, review your analytics to see how it performed compared to your other content. Use these insights to better serve your audience's preferences.

7. **Set Timeframes for Reflection**
   Schedule regular check-ins (e.g., monthly or quarterly) to assess your social media strategy. Reflect on what's working, what isn't, and how you can adjust your approach to stay aligned with your goals and audience needs.

8. **Engage with Your Audience**
   Set aside dedicated time each week to interact with your followers. Respond to comments, ask questions, or create polls to encourage engagement. Building relationships with your audience is more valuable than focusing solely on numbers.

9. **Stay Updated on Platform Changes**
   Dedicate a specific day each month to check for updates and trends on your chosen platforms.

Use this time to understand how changes might help you better connect with your audience, rather than viewing them as obstacles.

10. **Reflect on Your Brand's Evolution**
    Write a brief reflection on how your brand has evolved over the past few months. Consider any changes in your goals, content style, or audience engagement. Use these insights to inform your future strategy.

11. **Prioritize Self-Care**
    Remember to schedule time for yourself away from social media. Engage in activities that recharge you, ensuring you're approaching your strategy with a clear and positive mindset.

Sparkle 6: Branding – Shining in a Saturated World

Now that you've started settling into your personal brand's vibe, it's time to dive deeper into the art of standing out in a saturated world. Social media is crowded, and it's easy to feel like just another voice among millions. Every day, new creators are entering the space, talking about beauty, fitness, lifestyle, their pets, their food, their travels, you name it. But the question you need to ask yourself is: *What makes you truly unique?* The answer lies within you. You will always be you, and that in itself is powerful. Your uniqueness is something no one else can replicate. Your voice, your gestures, your experiences, and the way you connect with your audience are distinctly yours. These elements become a critical part of your branding and are key to setting you apart from the masses.

But here's the thing: standing out takes more than just being yourself—it requires intention and strategy. Authenticity alone is powerful, but pairing it with a clear, recognizable brand identity is what will make you memorable and, more importantly, recognizable. The truth is, people's attention spans are short, and the quicker they can identify your content as *yours*, the more you solidify your place in their minds. In a world where endless posts and stories are fighting for attention, your goal is to create a brand so distinct that when someone scrolls by your content, they already know it's you—even without checking the name attached.

The Power of Familiarity

Think about your favorite brands—whether it's a fashion label, a favorite podcast, or even a particular YouTuber. What keeps you coming back to them? It's likely the feeling you get every time you engage with their content. There's a sense of comfort in familiarity. When a brand consistently delivers on the vibe, look, and message that resonates with you, it creates a sense of connection. This connection isn't just accidental; it's built over time and nurtured through repetition.

As a content creator, this is your goal—to create a recognizable vibe that people connect with on an emotional level. When people associate your content with positive feelings, they will keep coming back for more. Your audience will start to anticipate the emotions and experiences they'll get from you. It's not just about what you post; it's about how your content makes them feel. And this is the essence of good branding. Your brand is an emotional experience as much as it is a visual one.

The Visual Identity: Creating Consistency

One of the easiest ways to become recognizable is by creating a consistent visual identity. This means establishing elements like fonts, colors, and designs that reflect both your personality and your message. Visual branding isn't just about looking pretty; it's about enhancing the emotions you want to evoke in your audience. When done correctly, your visual style should be so consistent that someone scrolling quickly can instantly say, "Oh, that's [your brand]," without even reading the post.

Let's start with **fonts**. Fonts are more powerful than people often realize. They can convey a tone—whether it's playful, professional, serious, or quirky. Choosing the right fonts is essential to communicating the vibe of your brand. The key here is to keep it simple. Stick to 2-4 fonts max. Your main font should be easy to read, as readability is crucial in a fast-paced digital world. You can get a little more creative with a secondary font for headings or special designs, but overall, consistency is queen. Using the same fonts repeatedly not only creates visual cohesion, but it also strengthens that sense of familiarity. Over time, these elements will become a recognizable part of your brand's DNA.

Now, let's talk about **colors**. Color is arguably one of the most emotionally charged aspects of branding. It's also where a lot of creators struggle because there are just so many to choose from! If you're like me, you might be tempted to use every color of the rainbow, but unfortunately, that approach will make your brand look chaotic and unfocused. Instead, stick to a cohesive palette that aligns with the feelings you want to evoke in your audience. Typically, you'll want two main colors and maybe one or two accent colors.

Here's a quick breakdown of some feelings associated with colors:

- **Red:** Passion, energy, urgency, love, strength.
- **Blue:** Calm, trust, dependability, intelligence, serenity.
- **Yellow:** Optimism, cheerfulness, creativity, warmth, positivity.
- **Green:** Growth, harmony, nature, balance, health, freshness.
- **Purple:** Luxury, wisdom, spirituality, creativity, mystery.
- **Black:** Power, sophistication, elegance, authority, formality.
- **White:** Simplicity, purity, cleanliness, peace, clarity.
- **Pink:** Compassion, warmth, playfulness, love, kindness.
- **Orange:** Enthusiasm, adventure, excitement, creativity, energy.

- **Gray:** Neutrality, balance, calm, professionalism, modernity.
- **Brown:** Stability, reliability, nature, warmth, earthiness.
- **Turquoise:** Clarity, healing, calm, balance, refreshment.
- **Gold:** Success, wealth, luxury, prestige, wisdom.
- **Silver:** Modernity, elegance, innovation, sleekness, high-tech.

Take some time to think about the emotions you want your audience to feel when they see your content. What colors are you naturally drawn to? Do these colors align with your brand's message and the emotions you're trying to evoke? It's not just about what looks good to you—it's about what *feels* right to your audience. The colors you choose should become a visual shorthand for your brand, helping to evoke the same feelings again and again as your audience engages with your content.

The Emotional Connection: Branding Beyond the Visual

Now that we've touched on the visuals, let's not forget that branding also goes beyond what people *see*. It extends into how you communicate and interact with your audience. Your tone of voice, the stories you share, the values you uphold—all of these become part of your brand. You want to create a space where your audience feels something every time they engage with you. Whether it's laughter, inspiration, comfort, or excitement, these emotional cues will shape how people perceive your brand.

For example, if your brand's personality is casual and upbeat, let that shine through in your captions, stories, and interactions. Speak like you're talking to a friend. On the other hand, if your brand is more professional and educational, your tone might be more informative and structured. Remember, your audience is drawn to you not just because of your content, but because of how you make them feel. These feelings create an emotional bond, and that bond is what will keep them coming back.

One powerful way to refine your brand's personality is by considering common archetypes. Archetypes are universal, recognizable character types that tap into the audience's emotional responses, helping you create a brand that resonates deeply. Swiss psychiatrist *Carl Jung* first introduced the idea of archetypes to describe patterns of behavior and personality that people instinctively understand and connect with. Today, branding experts use Jung's framework to help brands develop strong, relatable personalities that create lasting bonds with audiences. Here's a look at the 12 archetypes and how they might shape your brand's personality:

1. **The Caregiver** – Compassionate, nurturing, and empathetic, this brand seeks to make people feel safe, supported, and cared for. It's the friend who's always there to offer a helping hand, as seen in brands like *Johnson & Johnson*.

2. **The Hero** – Brave, determined, and driven to make a difference, the Hero inspires people to overcome challenges and pursue greatness. Brands like *Nike*, with their empowering "just do it" message, embody this archetype.

3. **The Jester** – Fun-loving, playful, and light-hearted, the Jester reminds people not to take life too seriously. It often uses humor to entertain and connect, much like *Old Spice*'s quirky, memorable advertising.

4. **The Sage** – Wise, knowledgeable, and analytical, the Sage seeks truth and insight, offering well-researched and valuable information. *Harvard Business Review* embodies the Sage by providing trusted and in-depth guidance.

5. **The Creator** – Imaginative, innovative, and original, the Creator's goal is to inspire people to dream and express themselves. Brands like *Adobe* reflect this archetype, encouraging creativity through their products and resources.

6. **The Innocent** – Optimistic, pure, and idealistic, the Innocent values happiness and simplicity,

promoting a world of peace and kindness. Brands like *Coca-Cola* align with this archetype, celebrating joy and positivity.

7. **The Ruler** – Confident, authoritative, and organized, the Ruler values control and stability, embodying leadership and reliability. Brands like *Rolex* and *Mercedes-Benz* represent this archetype, appealing to those who value structure and high quality.

8. **The Explorer** – Adventurous, independent, and curious, the Explorer seeks discovery and new experiences. Think of brands like *The North Face*, which encourages people to get out and explore the world.

9. **The Lover** – Passionate, warm, and committed, the Lover creates emotional connections and intimacy, drawing people in through sensory and romantic appeal. Brands like *Chanel* and *Godiva* reflect this archetype, evoking elegance and passion.

10. **The Magician** – Visionary, imaginative, and transformative, the Magician believes in endless possibilities and creates moments of wonder. *Disney* embodies this archetype by creating a sense of magic and enchantment in all it does.

11. **The Outlaw** – Bold, rebellious, and disruptive, the Outlaw challenges the status quo and embodies independence. Brands like

Harley-Davidson appeal to those who value freedom and self-expression.

12. **The Everyman** – Friendly, approachable, and relatable, the Everyman values belonging and community, appealing to a wide audience. *IKEA* represents the Everyman by making people feel at home with its inclusive and accessible products.

This list of archetypes is inspired by Carl Jung's archetype theory and has been adapted by branding experts to connect with modern audiences.

As you explore these archetypes, consider which traits naturally align with your personality and values. If you resonate with the Hero, for example, your tone might be bold and empowering, sharing motivational stories and encouraging your audience to take on new challenges. If you see yourself as the Jester, you might infuse humor and playfulness into your content, making your audience smile and feel at ease.

Ultimately, choosing an archetype (or sometimes two) helps you create a consistent brand identity that resonates on a deeper level. Whether you're channeling the optimism of the Caregiver, the drive of the Hero, the fun of the Jester, or the wisdom of the Sage, these personality traits offer a framework for connecting emotionally with your audience.

Remember, it's not just the content you share but the feeling you create that builds that all-important emotional bond. Let your brand's personality guide you as you engage with your community, building a unique voice that keeps them coming back.

Consistency is Key: Becoming a Recognizable Brand

The biggest challenge for any creator, especially one with a creative personality, is consistency. It's easy to get bored or to feel the pull to try new things, but remember—consistency breeds familiarity, and familiarity leads to trust. You want your audience to feel like they know you. They should be able to spot your content from a mile away and know it's you before even reading your name. That's when you know your brand is truly recognizable.

This doesn't mean you can't evolve or grow, but it does mean you should build a strong foundation first. Once you have your fonts, colors, and overall vibe established, stick to them. As tempting as it is to change things up frequently, resist the urge. The more consistent you are with your branding, the faster people will recognize your content and start associating it with the positive feelings you want them to experience.

Sparkle 6 Growth Tasks: Stand Out and Shine with Your Unique Brand Personality!

1. **Define Your Archetype and Vibe**
   Identify which of the 12 brand archetypes best represents your brand's core personality (like the Hero, Sage, or Jester) and write down three words that capture this vibe. For example, if you align with the Hero, your words might be "bold," "motivating," and "fearless." Let these words serve as a compass to guide your content style, voice, and audience interactions.

2. **Create a Personality-Focused Visual Mood Board**
   Gather images, colors, fonts, and textures that reflect not only the aesthetic but also the archetype-inspired personality you want to project. Tools like Pinterest or Canva are great for creating a mood board that represents the overall feeling of your brand's archetype. This will help keep your brand visually cohesive and reinforce your personality across platforms.

3. **Choose Your Color Palette with Emotional Impact**
   Select two primary colors and up to two accent colors that resonate with your archetype and brand message. Colors have emotional effects; for example, bold colors might suit the Hero, while soft pastels might fit the Innocent. Stick

with these colors for the next 30 days and notice how your audience responds emotionally.

4. **Select Fonts that Reflect Your Brand Personality**

   Choose one or two fonts that embody the tone of your archetype. For instance, a playful Jester brand might use a quirky, fun font, while a professional Sage might opt for classic, clean typography. Consistently use these fonts across your posts and graphics to establish a recognizable brand style.

5. **Analyze Your Existing Content for Personality Consistency**

   Scroll through your recent posts or videos and ask yourself: Are they reflecting the traits of your archetype? Are your images, colors, and tone aligned, or do they feel scattered? Identify where you can be more consistent in showcasing your brand personality, whether through visuals, captions, or overall mood.

6. **Audit Your Voice and Messaging for Brand Personality**

   Review recent captions, stories, or scripts. Do they communicate the qualities of your archetype? For example, if your archetype is the Sage, ensure your voice is informative and knowledgeable. Adjust your messaging to reinforce the emotional experience you want your audience to have when engaging with your brand.

7. **Create a One-Page Archetype Branding Guide**
   Write a simple, one-page branding guide that outlines your color palette, fonts, tone of voice, archetype, and core personality traits. This guide will keep you aligned as your brand grows. Use it every time you're creating content or designing graphics to maintain a strong, cohesive identity.

8. **Test, Tweak, and Reflect on Your Brand Evolution**
   After implementing your new branding elements and archetype-inspired style for a couple of months, observe how your audience engages. Do you notice more positive reactions or deeper connections? Take note of the feedback and make small adjustments to keep refining your brand.

9. **Invite Your Audience to Discover Your Brand Personality**
   Run a "Brand Personality Challenge" by posting a story or a poll asking your audience to describe your brand in three words. Are their responses aligned with your archetype and vibe? This feedback will give you insight into whether your brand personality is making the intended impact.

Sparkle 7: The Art of Connection – Building a Loyal Community

In the previous chapters, we explored the process of creating well-branded, intentional content for your audience. But now, it's time to talk about something else just as important: how to actively interact with your audience to build real, lasting relationships with the individuals who will form your loyal community. This chapter is all about connection—true, authentic connection—and how it can transform casual followers into dedicated supporters who not only value your content but become deeply invested in your journey.

We've touched on authenticity a lot already, but it's essential to understand that being authentic isn't just about what you create and share. Authenticity also extends to the relationships you build. It's one thing to craft authentic content and release it into the world, but to maintain a loyal group of followers who consistently engage with you and your content, you need to cultivate real, meaningful conversations with them. These are the people who will become the heartbeat of your community, who will cheer you on, and spread your message far and wide.

Building trust is the foundation of all this. When your audience feels that they can trust you—your intentions, your advice, your expertise—they will be more likely to not only listen, but to act. Trust invokes

loyalty, and that loyalty is the key to creating a
thriving community. When people trust you, they'll
engage more deeply with your content, share it with
others, and feel more inclined to support your
business or projects.

But I want to make one thing crystal clear: building
these relationships isn't about manipulation or profit.
It should never be driven solely by a desire for sales or
personal gain. Your primary goal should be driven by
your purpose, passion, and the unique gift you bring to
the world. Not everyone in your audience will buy
from you—and that's perfectly okay. In fact, most
won't. But those who do will do so with enthusiasm,
because they believe in you and what you stand for.
These people will become your greatest advocates,
sharing your message with others through the most
powerful marketing tool of all: word of mouth.

Think about it—if your best friend opened a new salon,
you wouldn't just consider them for your next haircut;
you'd likely cheer them on, tell your friends about it,
and feel genuinely excited for their success. Why?
Because you trust them, you know their story, and
their journey feels personal to you. That's the essence
of genuine connection. The same principle applies
online, but it's not as straightforward. Through a
screen, building trust and connection takes more
effort because people are naturally cautious. After all,
they've been exposed to so many polished, filtered,

and inauthentic personas that they might doubt the realness of anyone's intentions.

This can feel discouraging at times, but here's the truth: authenticity stands out. When your audience senses that you're truly *you*—sharing your highs and lows, showing up with sincerity, and consistently offering value—they'll begin to trust you. Over time, the right people will see the real you, and that's when the magic happens. They won't just see you as a creator; they'll see you as a person worth rooting for.

This isn't about quick transactions; it's about creating a space where people feel connected, inspired, and understood. Yes, it takes time and persistence, but the rewards are unmatched. Those who stay true to themselves and nurture their community through thick and thin are the ones who truly thrive. Genuine connection may not happen overnight, but when it does, it becomes the foundation of something lasting and powerful.

Navigating Digital Relationships

Now, you might be wondering, "How do we build these important friendships in a digital world where face-to-face interactions are rare? How can we create those strong bonds when we can't just grab coffee or have a girls' night out?"

This is where the power of video and social media communication comes in. Video, especially live streams and stories, can bridge that gap and make you more real and relatable to your audience. It brings out your personality in ways that static images or text cannot. But even more important than the video itself is the conversation that follows. The way you engage in the comments section, respond to DMs, and interact with your followers can make or break your connection with them.

It's not enough to just post content and hope for the best. Engagement is a two-way street. If someone takes the time to comment on your posts or videos, that's an opportunity for connection that you don't want to waste. Failing to reply to your audience is like someone walking up to you in real life, saying hello, and you completely ignoring them. It's a surefire way to lose potential relationships, customers, and supporters. Even if it's a simple "thank you," showing that you're paying attention and value their interaction.

Of course, not all comments will be positive. Occasionally, you'll face negative comments, and how you handle them will set the tone for the kind of community you build. My advice? Stay calm, stay kind, and stay professional. Responding with maturity and positivity will not only diffuse the situation but also show your broader audience that you are grounded and respectful, even in the face of negativity. On the other hand, if the comment is offensive or harmful, don't hesitate to delete it—creating a positive space for your community is essential, and sometimes that means setting firm boundaries.

The Power of DMs: Meaningful Conversations Matter

If there's one tool in your digital communication toolbox that you should be using consistently, it's direct messages (DMs). DMs provide a more personal, intimate way to connect with your audience beyond public comments. And here's something many people don't realize: strong DM interactions can actually boost your overall engagement. Social media algorithms prioritize showing content from accounts with whom users have frequent, meaningful interactions, and DMs are a major factor in this.

That said, DMing should never feel cold or transactional. The key to starting conversations via DMs is to keep it genuine and authentic. Avoid the trap of sending copy-pasted messages or 'cold DMing' potential followers with business pitches right off the bat. There are much more effective, and authentic, ways to build relationships through direct messaging.

A great way to start a DM conversation is to simply thank someone for following you—it's easy, thoughtful, and makes them feel seen. From there, keep it light and friendly. You could say something like, "Hey, thanks for following! I'd love to hear—what kind of content do you enjoy most?" or "What brought you to my page? I always love to know what inspires people to connect!" These kinds of questions aren't about pitching or selling; they're about learning what they care about and showing you're interested in them as a real person. The goal is to create a space where they feel comfortable sharing, not to push an agenda. Authenticity always leads to better connections.

Another fantastic way to spark meaningful DM conversations is by responding to someone's story. This is my personal favorite way to start conversations. Stories are like glimpses into people's daily lives—their unfiltered moments, passions, or just little snippets of their day. When you reply to something they've shared, you're not just starting a conversation; you're letting them know you see and appreciate *them*. It's such a simple way to show genuine interest.

For instance, if they post a picture of their homemade meal, you could comment with, "That looks amazing! Is the recipe easy to make?" Or if they share a photo from a hike, try saying, "Wow, where is that? It looks like such a peaceful spot!" Compliments are also a great way to engage—commenting on a cute outfit, a creative project, or even their pet shows you're paying attention to the details.

This approach works so well because it feels natural and effortless. You're not coming in with an agenda or trying to make it about you. Instead, you're acknowledging *them* and creating space for a genuine back-and-forth. It's these organic moments of connection that build trust and deepen relationships, turning casual followers into real friends or loyal community members.

The beauty of responding to stories is that the conversation flows naturally. It's less about planning what to say and more about responding in the moment. That authenticity shines through and makes your interaction feel more like chatting with a friend than anything else.

Lastly, don't be afraid to create opportunities for people to DM you! A popular tactic among influencers is to create posts that invite audience members to reach out. For instance, you might offer a free guide or resource and ask them to DM you a specific word to receive it. This not only opens up a conversation but also gives you a chance to deliver value right away.

Email Lists: Your Secret Weapon for Long-Term Connection

As much as social media is a powerful tool, there's one aspect of digital marketing that often gets overlooked: email. Unlike social media platforms, where algorithms control who sees your posts, emails go directly to your audience's inbox. And guess what? People are more likely to open an email than to come across your latest Instagram post. That personal connection is invaluable.

Building an email list should be a priority from the start of your influencer journey. Even if your social media presence grows and thrives, an email list is something you own. Platforms can change, accounts can be hacked or lost, but your email list remains yours, and it's a direct line to your most dedicated fans.

You can start growing your email list by offering freebies or valuable resources in exchange for email addresses. This could be a downloadable guide, a checklist, or a mini-course—anything that aligns with your audience's interests and provides them with value. This not only helps you grow your list but also strengthens your connection by giving your audience something useful, further solidifying your relationship.

Take the Leap: Hosting Local Meetups

If it aligns with your brand and you can do so safely, hosting a local meetup can be a powerful way to deepen the connections you've built online. There's something truly special about taking relationships offline and creating a space where your community can gather in person. Whether you're in a bustling city with countless coffee shops or a smaller town where the community feels tighter-knit, a local meetup can bring your audience closer together and strengthen your bond with them.

If you're in a larger city, consider meeting at a trendy coffee shop, a local park, or a co-working space that's easy to access and has a friendly vibe. If you're in a smaller town, hosting something at a local café, library, or even a community center can make your gathering feel cozy and personal. The key is to choose a venue that feels welcoming and aligns with the tone of your community.

When planning your meetup, think about the experience you want to create. Keep it casual and approachable—this isn't about putting on a big production but about fostering real connections. When you arrive, make sure you're in a positive and genuine mindset. Greet everyone warmly, spend time chatting with each person, and make them feel valued. First impressions matter, and showing up as your authentic self will leave a lasting impact.

In-person vibes are unmatched when it comes to relationship-building. They allow people to see and feel your energy in a way that simply can't be replicated online. Whether it's sharing laughs, swapping stories, or brainstorming ideas, these moments create memories that strengthen your community's foundation.

If a local meetup feels like too big of a step right now, start small. Maybe it's hosting a virtual coffee chat over Zoom, replying more thoughtfully to DMs, or sending a voice note to a loyal follower. Write down your plan, execute it, and reflect on how it made both you and your audience feel. Remember, connections don't have to be grand gestures—they just have to be real.

Sparkle 7 Growth Tasks for Building a Loyal Community:

1. **Engage with Five Followers Today**
   Take the time to reply to five recent comments on your posts or videos. Make sure your responses are thoughtful, not just generic replies. Try asking a follow-up question or adding value to the conversation.

2. **Start Genuine Conversations in DMs**
   Reach out to three new followers in your DMs today. Thank them for following and ask them a question like, "What brought you to my page?" or "What type of content do you enjoy the most?" Keep it conversational, not sales-driven.

3. **Respond to Five Stories**
   Scroll through your followers' Instagram or Facebook stories and reply to at least five of them with genuine interest. This is a great way to start conversations naturally.

4. **Create a Call-to-Action Post**
   Make a post that invites your audience to DM you a specific word to receive a free resource (like a checklist or mini guide). This not only provides value but opens the door for one-on-one conversations with your followers.

5. **Develop a Freebie to Build Your Email List**
   Create a simple freebie (e.g., a PDF guide or

checklist) that aligns with your niche, and use it to start building your email list. Announce it on your social media platforms and offer it in exchange for email signups.

6. **Reply to a Negative Comment with Positivity**
    If you receive any negative comments, try replying in a calm, positive, and professional way. Use this as a chance to practice how you'll handle negativity while staying true to your values.

7. **Set a Weekly Engagement Goal**
    Establish a goal for yourself to engage meaningfully with a set number of followers each week—whether it's responding to comments, DMs, or participating in their content. Track your progress and reflect on how it strengthens your community.

8. **Create a Poll or Question Sticker in Your Stories**
    Post a poll or question in your Instagram stories to encourage interaction. Ask for feedback, opinions, or preferences related to your content. Engage with the responses to keep the conversation going.

Sparkle 8: Overcoming the Algorithm – The Technical Side of Growth

Dun Dun Dun!! The dreaded algorithm! It sounds like something lurking in the shadows, controlling your every social media move, right? But here's the good news: don't get scared, and don't get overwhelmed. As I've emphasized throughout this book, the algorithm is ever-changing and should not be a source of stress. Think of it less like a mysterious force and more like a tool. Once you understand its general purpose, you'll start seeing it as something you can work *with* rather than something you're up against.

Let's break it down. The purpose of algorithms on social media platforms is to ensure that people are seeing content that keeps them engaged, entertained, or informed. These platforms are businesses, after all, and their success depends on keeping users around for as long as possible. The longer people spend scrolling, the more ads they'll see, and that means more revenue for the platform. So the algorithm's main job is to make sure users keep coming back for more content they love.

So, where do *you* come in? Simple: you need to focus on adding value to your audience, through entertainment, education, or inspiration. The more valuable your content, the more likely it is that the algorithm will notice and push it to more people. But what does "value" really mean, and how do you achieve it?

Quality Over Quantity – It's Not About Fancy Gear

When we talk about adding value, many people automatically assume that they need top-tier production value—fancy cameras, professional lighting setups, the works. But let me tell you, many of the most successful creators are simply using their smartphones and a dash of creativity! Quality content is not about expensive equipment; it's about the intentional thought and care you put into your posts. It's about whether your content genuinely connects with your audience.

Think back to the idea of content pillars that we discussed in Chapter 5. Your pillars should guide every piece of content you produce, ensuring it aligns with the core themes and values you want to share with your audience. If you're sticking to those pillars, your content is going to resonate, and that's what matters most. If you're churning out multiple posts a day but they lack focus or intention, you're only hurting your chances. The algorithm might notice the quantity, but it rewards quality and engagement. Consistent, valuable content is key.

Another reason sticking to your pillars is so powerful is that it helps the algorithm figure out who would want to see your content. Algorithms thrive on patterns, using data about audience behavior to decide what to push out next. When your content is focused and consistent, it's easier for the algorithm to match it with the right people—the ones most likely to engage, follow, and stick around. Over time, this process fine-tunes your audience, ensuring that the people who see your posts are the ones who will genuinely love them.

On the other hand, if your content is scattered across unrelated topics, it sends mixed signals. The algorithm can't narrow down who your ideal audience is, and your posts may end up reaching people who aren't interested. This not only wastes effort but also reduces the likelihood of building a loyal, engaged community. Staying true to your content pillars allows the algorithm to work in your favor, making it a powerful ally in connecting you with the perfect audience for your brand.

Consistency – Your Trust with the Algorithm

Consistency is one of the biggest factors that algorithms look for. You don't need to post ten times a day or even every day at all to be successful. What's important is that you create a pattern that the algorithm (and your audience) can trust. Think of consistency like a rhythm. The platform wants to see that you're showing up regularly. Whether you can commit to posting three times a week or once every day, it's all about being reliable.

The algorithm is designed to reward creators who appear consistently because it signals to the platform that you're dependable. This, in turn, helps the platform feel confident in showing your content to more people over time. Think of it like a partnership: the algorithm pushes your content because it trusts that you'll be around to keep engaging with your audience.

But here's the thing: don't fall into the trap of pushing yourself to the point of burnout in the name of consistency. You need to create a schedule that fits your lifestyle and mental health. If you can only post twice a week, that's completely fine. Just make sure you show up for those two days, every week. Consistency isn't about frequency; it's about reliability.

Mental Health and Burnout – Pace Yourself for Longevity

Speaking of burnout, let's pause for a second and address something critical: your well-being. It's easy to feel pressure to churn out content at a breakneck pace, especially when you see other creators posting constantly. But remember, every creator's journey is different. Your mental health and long-term sustainability are far more important than chasing daily posts.

Social media is a marathon, not a sprint. If you push yourself too hard too fast, you'll burn out—and when that happens, it can take a serious toll on both your creativity and your engagement. It's okay to take breaks. It's okay to post less often. What's important is that you're consistent within your own capacity and that you protect your mental well-being. If you can only manage to post once a week, own that! Your audience will appreciate your authenticity, and the algorithm will reward your reliability over time.

Scheduling Content – Your Secret Weapon for Consistency

One of the best tools at your disposal for staying consistent is scheduling your content in advance. Most platforms today offer built-in scheduling tools, so you don't even need to download anything extra to make this work. And the beauty of scheduling is that it allows you to create content in batches—meaning you can dedicate one weekend a month to content creation and have an entire month's worth of posts ready to go.

Imagine the relief of knowing that your content is showing up for your audience even when you're taking a break or focusing on other aspects of your business. Scheduling takes the pressure off while allowing you to remain consistent. But there's one warning: while your posts may be automated, your engagement can't be. You still need to show up to interact with your audience. Building relationships with your followers is just as important as posting regularly, and it's something that no scheduling tool can replace.

Engagement – It's a Two-Way Street

You've probably heard it said a thousand times: "Engagement is key." And it's true! Engagement is what fuels the algorithm's decision-making. If people are liking, commenting, and sharing your content, that sends a strong signal to the platform that your posts are worth sharing with a wider audience.

But don't think of engagement as just a numbers game. As we discussed in the last chapter, it's a two-way street. Yes, you want people to engage with your content, but you also need to be engaging with them. Take time to respond to comments, ask your audience questions, and interact with their content too. These small actions build community and trust, both with your audience and the algorithm. When the platform sees that you're actively participating in conversations, it rewards you by boosting your content. This might be the most important reason pillars are so important as well, when the right audience sees your content they will be more likely to engage, which means you'll be more likely to build a valuable relationship. It's a win-win all around. When we start viewing the algorithm this way, it's a lot harder to be so upset with it. In fact, the more I learn about algorithms, the more I actually love them. It's helping my ideal audience find me! It's not working against me, it's working for both me and my audience so we can come together. The only people it works against are those just pushing out mindless content. Being intentional benefits everyone and gives a lot more meaning to the lives involved.

The Evolving Nature of Algorithms – Stay Adaptable

Finally, one last word on algorithms: they're always evolving. What works today may not work six months from now, and that's okay! You don't need to stress about every update or change. As long as you stay true to the core principles of adding value, remaining consistent, and engaging with your community, you'll always be able to adapt.

In fact, adaptability is one of the most valuable skills you can have as a content creator. Don't get stuck in your ways or become overly reliant on any one method or strategy. Stay curious, keep experimenting, and be willing to adjust your approach when necessary. Remember, the algorithm may change, but your commitment to your audience and your message should remain constant.

Sparkle 8 Growth Tasks: Overcoming the Algorithm

1. **Evaluate Your Content Quality:** Review your last 10 posts. Are they aligned with your content pillars? Do they add value—whether through education, entertainment, or inspiration? If not, brainstorm ways to create more intentional, valuable content for your audience.

2. **Create a Consistency Plan:** Decide on a posting schedule that works for you. Can you post once a day? Twice a week? Whatever feels sustainable, commit to it for at least the next month. Remember, consistency is key, not frequency.

3. **Batch and Schedule Content:** Set aside a block of time (e.g., one weekend or a few hours a week) to create and schedule content in advance. Most platforms offer scheduling features, or you can use tools like Buffer, Later, or Hootsuite. This will help you stay consistent without daily stress.

4. **Engage with Your Audience:** For every post, spend at least 15–30 minutes responding to comments and engaging with your followers. Build genuine relationships by asking questions, offering support, and being part of the conversation.

5. **Track Your Engagement Metrics:** Pay attention to which posts are getting the most likes, comments, and shares. Are there any patterns in the types of content that perform well? Use this data to tweak your strategy and focus on what resonates most with your audience.

6. **Stay Adaptable:** Dedicate time each month to learn about updates or changes to the platform's algorithm. Watch tutorials, read articles, and keep an eye on what's working for other creators. Stay flexible, and don't be afraid to adjust your strategy when necessary.

Sparkle 9: Dealing with Negativity – Staying Positive in a Critical World

Social media can be a beautiful space—a place to share positivity, knowledge, and inspiration. However, while your content may focus on uplifting others and giving back to the world with positive influence, not everyone is on the same page. Unfortunately, the online world also harbors its fair share of criticism, comparison, and negativity. Being behind a screen makes people feel safe enough to say things they probably wouldn't say face-to-face.

In the words of Taylor Swift, "Say it in the streets, it's a knock-out, but say it in a tweet, it's a cop-out." Her lyrics show the reality that many people feel like they have the courage to lash out from behind their keyboards. It's easy to throw negativity out there when there's no immediate consequence or accountability. And yes, we can't forget her famous line, "Haters gonna hate, hate, hate, hate, hate," which applies to social media like never before. It's part of the experience, but the trick is not letting it define yours.

Acknowledging the Uncontrollable

Let's take a moment to acknowledge that no matter how hard you try, you cannot control what happens beyond yourself. It's a tough pill to swallow, but understanding this early on will save you a lot of mental anguish. The way someone reacts to your post—whether they love it or hate it—is ultimately a reflection of them, not you. Their perception is filtered through their experiences, biases, and emotions. You are responsible for creating content with integrity and positivity, but beyond that, you must let go of the outcome.

The real challenge is learning to stay centered in your own truth when negativity arises. Should you really let someone else's passing judgment or negative comment hold enough power to make you second-guess yourself? Absolutely not. By giving weight to their words, you are handing over your power, allowing their negativity to dim your light. As difficult as it may be, the best response is to continue standing in your truth and shining in your authenticity. You are on this journey to help others, to give a good message, and to spread positivity. Don't let a few naysayers derail your mission.

Navigating Hot-Button Topics

While it's important to speak from the heart and share what's important to you, it's equally important to choose your battles wisely. One area to tread lightly in is politics. Unless your page is specifically about political commentary or social justice, diving into political discussions can quickly take the energy of your page in a negative direction. Politics, as we all know, can be polarizing, and no matter how much positivity you infuse into the conversation, some people will see it as an invitation to argue.

There's a reason many influencers steer clear of political discourse—it's not about shying away from important topics but rather maintaining the tone and energy you've worked hard to create. If your brand is built on positivity, connection, and upliftment, getting into divisive debates can disrupt the community you've cultivated. Yes, you may experience a spike in engagement, but at what cost? You want to bring people together, not create a divide. Many will unfollow if you start sharing political views (myself included), and you may find the atmosphere on your page quickly turns combative. Stay true to your core message, and ask yourself if certain discussions align with the vibe you're curating.

Handling Negative Comments with Grace

Negative comments are inevitable. It's not a question of *if*, but *when* they will show up. When they do, how you respond is crucial. A calm, professional approach speaks volumes not only to the person commenting but also to your wider audience. People are watching how you handle adversity, and this is a key opportunity to reinforce your values and character.

If a comment is outright hateful, offensive, or discriminatory, don't hesitate to delete it. Your page is a space where you set the tone, and you are under no obligation to entertain toxic energy. For instance, if someone leaves a comment full of discriminatory language or personal attacks, removing it immediately and, if necessary, blocking the individual ensures that your platform remains a safe, inclusive space. Everyone should feel welcome.

However, if it's a genuine complaint or even just a criticism, consider it an opportunity to turn the situation around. For example, someone might comment, "The product didn't arrive on time, and I'm really disappointed," or "I don't agree with what you said in your post—it felt dismissive." These are chances to engage thoughtfully and demonstrate that you value your audience's input. Respond calmly, such as:

- *"I'm so sorry to hear about the delay! This isn't the experience we want for our customers. Can you send me a direct message with your order details? I'd love to look into this for you and make it right."*
- *"Thank you for sharing your perspective. It's never my intention to make anyone feel dismissed. Could you share more about how you interpreted my post? I'd like to better understand and clarify my message."*

Showing empathy and a willingness to address the issue demonstrates professionalism and care. A thoughtful response not only resolves the concern but also shows others in your community that you take feedback seriously.

People appreciate honesty and humility. If something does go wrong—perhaps a product doesn't work as promised or your message wasn't clear—own it. For instance, if someone says, "I bought this because of your recommendation, but it didn't work for me," a response like, *"I'm sorry to hear that it didn't meet your expectations! Let's discuss your experience and see if we can find a solution or a product that works better for you,"* can transform a negative situation into a positive one.

Similarly, if a post unintentionally offends someone, respond by acknowledging their feelings:

- *"I truly regret that my words came across that way—it was never my goal to make anyone feel excluded. Thank you for pointing this out, and I'll be more mindful in the future."*

Admitting mistakes and correcting them builds trust. When people feel heard and valued, they are more likely to stick around, even if their initial experience wasn't perfect. By responding with sincerity and a commitment to improvement, you demonstrate integrity and create stronger connections with your audience.

Avoiding the Comparison Trap

Comparison is one of the most dangerous pitfalls in the digital world. It's easy to look at other influencers in your niche and wonder why they seem to be growing faster, why they have more followers, or why their content looks so polished. This is the trap: comparing your beginning to someone else's middle or even end.

What you see on social media is only a snapshot, a highlight reel of someone's life and career. You don't know the behind-the-scenes struggles, the years of hard work, or the resources they have. Maybe they've been at it for much longer than you, or perhaps they had a built-in audience from another platform. It's impossible to know all the variables that contributed to their success. Instead of focusing on someone else's journey, stay committed to your own.

One way to combat comparison is to keep a visible list of your strengths and your "why." Why did you start this journey? What is your unique gift to the world? By keeping these reminders close, you can ground yourself in your mission whenever doubt creeps in. You are on your own path, and that path is valid. You are serving your purpose, just as they are serving theirs. The digital world is vast enough for all of us to thrive in our own lanes.

It's also important to remember that two people in the same niche can share a similar message, but because you are both unique individuals, you'll attract similar audiences for entirely different reasons. Your voice, experiences, and personality create a connection that's distinctly yours. Instead of viewing others as competition, consider them as potential collaborators. Reaching out to someone with a similar audience and size could lead to meaningful partnerships where you both grow together by sharing ideas, creativity, and audiences.

When you collaborate rather than compete, you amplify your mission and invite others to join in. If you truly stand behind your purpose, consider that others in your community feel the same. Together, you could create something even more impactful—a passion project that combines your unique strengths and furthers your shared message. After all, the digital space thrives on connection, and there's power in building each other up rather than tearing each other down.

Taking Mental Health Breaks

With all the pressure and constant connectivity, taking care of your mental health is non-negotiable.

Obviously, I'm bringing this up in many chapters, but I am going to drill it into your habits however I can. It's easy to get caught up in the grind of creating content, keeping up with trends, and maintaining your engagement. But remember this: you can't pour from an empty cup. If you feel your energy depleting or your mood shifting negatively, take a step back. There is power in knowing when to disconnect.

Schedule some content ahead of time, then give yourself permission to unplug. Take a walk outside, breathe in the fresh air, hydrate, and move your body. Your physical and mental well-being are essential not just for you, but for the work you do. How can you continue to uplift and inspire others if you're running on empty? Living your message is as important as sharing it. I've had some of my most creative and successful ideas come to me while I was taking a day off to relax. When you're really forced to do nothing, your brain has the space to come up with all kinds of great ideas. Plus, by taking care of yourself, you are leading by example, showing people that living a balanced life is actually possible if you are willing to slow down some of your days.

In a world that often glorifies hustle culture, taking a break can feel like failure, but it's far from it. Your worth isn't determined by how much you produce, but by who you are. You are valuable simply because you exist, and your contribution to this world is meaningful. So, take that rest, recharge your spirit, and come back stronger. Your audience will appreciate the authentic energy you bring when you return, refreshed and renewed.

Shining in the Darkness

The online world can feel overwhelming at times, filled with shadows that threaten to dull your brilliance. But remember, light thrives in darkness—it doesn't shrink to fit its surroundings. Instead of dimming yourself to make others more comfortable, let your authenticity and passion shine brighter. Flood your corner of the internet with positivity and proudly share the wonderful things that make your voice unique.

Your purpose isn't just to navigate this space but to transform it, one post, one connection, one moment at a time. Stay rooted in your mission, offer value with intention, and let the negativity slip past you like waves on the shore. The world is watching, not just for entertainment but for inspiration, for hope, for a reason to believe in the good things again.

You are an influencer not because of numbers, but because of your actions. By living the positivity you wish to see, you spark a ripple effect. You empower others to be courageous, to be kind, to be unapologetically themselves. So, keep shining—boldly, brightly, and without apology. The world needs your light more than ever.

Sparkle 9 Growth Tasks: Dealing with Negativity and Staying Positive

1. **Create a Positive Mantra:** Develop a personal mantra or affirmation that you can repeat to yourself when negativity arises. Examples: "I am confident in my voice," or "Other people's opinions don't define my worth." Write it down somewhere visible or save it as your phone wallpaper to remind yourself daily.
2. **Respond with Kindness:** The next time you receive a negative or critical comment, challenge yourself to respond calmly and positively. Before replying, take a moment to breathe, reflect, and approach the situation with empathy. If it's a genuine critique, offer a solution; if it's negativity for the sake of it, respond with grace or delete if necessary.
3. **Unfollow or Mute Accounts that Trigger Comparison:** Go through your social media following list and identify any accounts that consistently make you feel "less than." It could be that the content doesn't align with your values or that it triggers self-doubt. Don't hesitate to unfollow or mute these accounts to protect your mental well-being.
4. **Write a Gratitude List:** Reflect on what you've achieved so far in your journey. Write down at least five things you're grateful for about your

personal growth or the positive impact you've had on your community. Keep this list somewhere easy to access, so you can look back on it whenever comparison or negativity starts to creep in.

5. **Set Boundaries for Screen Time**: Schedule regular breaks from social media to recharge and refresh. Create a plan for how often you'll take "digital detox" days or even a few hours away from the screen. During these breaks, focus on activities that nourish your mind and body, such as exercise, reading, or spending time with loved ones.

6. **Celebrate Small Wins**: Identify a recent accomplishment, no matter how small, and share it with your audience or journal about it. Shifting focus to positive achievements helps maintain a healthy mindset and reinforces the impact you're having, despite any negative feedback.

7. **Turn Off Notifications**: If the constant buzz of notifications makes you feel anxious or overwhelmed, set aside specific times during the day to check social media instead of being constantly plugged in. This helps you stay in control of your online engagement rather than being reactive to every comment or message.

8. **Start a Positivity Journal**: At the end of each day, write down one positive interaction or

piece of feedback you received. It could be a compliment, a kind comment, or a personal milestone. On tough days, revisit your positivity journal to remind yourself of all the good your content brings into the world.

Sparkle 10: Self-Care for Influencers – Balancing Growth and Wellness

In the fast-paced world of influencing, where content creation, community engagement, and brand partnerships can take up the bulk of your time, self-care often gets pushed to the bottom of the priority list. However, the key to long-term success in this space isn't just about producing viral posts or gaining followers—it's about finding balance and prioritizing wellness. The most effective way to ensure you are caring for yourself as an influencer is through intentional time management that allows space for both growth and rest. Without this balance, burnout is inevitable.

Burnout isn't just about feeling tired; it's a state of emotional, physical, and mental exhaustion caused by prolonged stress. And once you reach that point, it's much harder to recover. Preventing burnout starts with recognizing that your well-being is just as important as hitting those follower goals. It's about blocking time not only for work but for essential aspects of your life that fuel your creativity and motivation—like physical movement, quality sleep, meaningful relationships, and activities that bring you joy.

It's tempting to think that the hustle mindset is the only path to success—that if you just push a little harder, grind a little longer, you'll achieve your goals faster. But the truth is, real growth comes from a place of balance. A truly successful influencer isn't just someone who checks off their to-do list; it's someone who radiates energy, who sustains their momentum by taking care of themselves. It's about living a life that others aspire to, not because of your follower count, but because of how you manage to "do it all" with grace and ease.

The Importance of Slowing Down

It's ironic, but one of the best-kept secrets of productivity is learning to slow down. In a world that tells us to hustle, to always be "on," slowing down might feel counterintuitive. However, it's in those moments of rest and reflection that your best ideas come to life. When you're always rushing from one task to the next, your creativity and mental clarity suffer. Slowing down gives you the chance to be present—not only for your audience but for yourself.

When you allow yourself the time to enjoy a peaceful morning routine or take a break for an afternoon walk, you're not being lazy; you're recharging. These moments of intentional downtime help clear your mind and boost your energy so that when you return to your work, you're focused, refreshed, and ready to tackle whatever comes your way. You might even find that by pacing yourself, you're able to accomplish

more, because you're operating from a place of
mindfulness rather than exhaustion.

Making Self-Care Non-Negotiable

Taking care of yourself is not a luxury—it's a necessity.
Without self-care, it becomes increasingly difficult to
maintain the high energy levels that the influencer
world demands. It's easy to get caught up in the
whirlwind of responsibilities: juggling content
creation, partnerships, family obligations, and
maintaining friendships. Add to that the pressure to
keep up appearances both online and offline, and
self-care starts to feel like just another chore.

When you do finally carve out some time for yourself,
you might find that you're too drained to actually
enjoy it. Something as simple as doing your skincare
routine at the end of the day or squeezing in a short
walk can feel overwhelming when you're already burnt
out. But here's the thing—self-care doesn't have to be
complicated. It's not about spending hours at a spa or
doing an elaborate routine every night. It's about
committing to small, meaningful actions that make
you feel good and remind you that you're worth the
time and effort.

At first, these actions might feel hard, especially when
you're running on fumes. Washing your face when
you'd rather collapse into bed, or doing a quick stretch

when you've been sitting all day, might feel like a
burden. But over time, these small habits will start to
pay off. They'll give you the energy to tackle bigger
tasks and will shift your mindset from one of
exhaustion to one of empowerment. Think about a
habit like brushing your teeth. As a child, you might
have fought against it—dragging your feet and needing
constant reminders from your parents. But now, it's
second nature; you do it without even thinking
because you've internalized its importance. As adults,
we can create new habits just like this. It requires us to
be intentional and, unlike childhood, we don't have
parents making us stick to it when we'd rather not.
Instead, we must build self-discipline. By committing
to these small, life-changing habits, we can transform
not only our routines but also the way we approach
our day-to-day lives.

Self-care is the physical manifestation of self-love.
While affirmations and positive thinking are powerful
tools for building confidence, it's your actions that
speak loudest. Taking the time to care for your body,
mind, and soul is an act of love and respect toward
yourself. So if you've been skipping out on self-care,
start small. Add one new habit at a time and watch
how it begins to transform not just your energy but
your overall sense of well-being.

The Power of Time Management

Time management isn't just about getting more done; it's about getting the right things done while preserving your energy and well-being. As we discussed earlier in the book, time blocking is an invaluable tool for staying organized and focused. But it's not just about blocking out time for work-related tasks—it's about ensuring that your schedule reflects a balanced life.

One way to bring more awareness to how you spend your time is by using color coding in your planner. Assign different colors to various areas of your life—green for work, blue for family, pink for self-care, yellow for health, and so on. This visual representation will give you a clear picture of how balanced (or imbalanced) your life truly is. If you look at your calendar and see that it's mostly green, you'll know you've been overworking. If you don't see any pink at all, it's a sign that you've been neglecting self-care.

Balance is a visual cue that can help you stay accountable to yourself. It also serves as a reminder that while work is important, it's not the only thing that matters. It's in those moments of self-care, family time, and health maintenance that you actually refuel your ability to work more effectively.

Journaling: A Simple Yet Powerful Tool

Another powerful self-care practice that often gets overlooked is journaling. It feels like one of those self-care tips that's over-shared, but in reality it's just *that* important, and it's mind blowing how little people actually give writing in a journal their time. Writing down your thoughts, feelings, and experiences at the end of each day is a great way to unwind and process everything that's going on in your life. Journaling helps you gain insight into your own patterns, highlights where you're thriving, and reveals areas where you might need more support. It also serves as a form of release, allowing you to empty your mind of any lingering thoughts before heading to bed.

The beauty of journaling is that it doesn't have to be time-consuming or perfect. Some nights, you might only jot down a single sentence, while other nights you may feel the need to pour out your thoughts in a long, reflective entry. Both are equally valuable. By making journaling a habit, you give yourself the space to check in with yourself regularly, which is crucial as you continue to grow your business and navigate the complexities of both your online and offline life.

As your influence expands, so will your responsibilities. Journaling can help you manage feelings of overwhelm by offering clarity and focus. It's a simple act, but one that can have a profound impact on how you approach both your personal life and your career.

Wellness as a Foundation for Success

The influencer lifestyle can be incredibly rewarding, but it can also be taxing if you don't prioritize your well-being. Success isn't just about hitting your growth targets—it's about sustaining your energy and enthusiasm for the long haul. By weaving self-care practices into your daily routine, you're setting yourself up for sustained growth—both in your career and in your personal life.

It's important to remember that self-care isn't selfish. It's the foundation upon which everything else is built. Without it, your ability to create, connect, and inspire will slowly diminish. But when you nurture your body, mind, and spirit, you'll find that you have more to give—to your audience, your family, and most importantly, to yourself.

You can also consider integrating wellness into both your content and daily life if it makes sense with your personal brand. Consider what kind of self-care aligns with your values, your message, and even your audience. Self-care is not one-size-fits-all—it's deeply personal and can reflect the lifestyle you're sharing with others. Here are some practical ways to incorporate and showcase self-care that resonates:

1. Aligning Self-Care with Your Brand

- If your brand emphasizes creativity, try sharing practices like journaling, mindful coloring, or nature walks to spark inspiration.
- If your niche involves physical health or beauty, show behind-the-scenes moments of your skincare routine, workout sessions, or preparing nourishing meals.
- For mental health and positivity-focused brands, highlight meditation, affirmations, or digital detox days.

By aligning self-care with your personal brand, you not only stay authentic to the self care you need, but also connect with your audience on a deeper level.

2. Engaging Your Audience in Wellness Discussions

Your audience can be a source of inspiration when discovering new wellness practices.

- **Polls and Q&A Sessions:** Use your platform to ask your followers about their favorite self-care rituals. Not only will this boost engagement, but it may also introduce you to new ideas that resonate with you and your community.
- **Share and Invite Participation:** For example, you could host a "30 Days of Self-Care"

challenge where you and your audience explore different activities together.

3. Practical Tools for Personal Growth and Self-Care

Consider integrating tools that help make self-care more accessible:

- **Apps:** Introduce meditation apps, habit trackers, or wellness/fitness apps.
- **Journaling Templates:** Share downloadable templates for gratitude journaling or goal-setting that your followers can use.
- **Books and Podcasts:** Recommend resources that have helped you grow, such as books on mindfulness or podcasts on work-life balance.

4. Showcase Your Journey

Your audience connects with you because of your story. Don't be afraid to share your wins, challenges, and how self-care is helping you grow. Whether it's trying a new workout class or learning to set boundaries, your journey can inspire others to prioritize themselves too.

By taking time to explore what self-care means to you—and to your audience—you're doing more than maintaining your own wellness; you're leading by example. You're showing that success isn't just about

numbers or aesthetics; it's about living a life that feels
good from the inside out. When you prioritize
self-care as part of your growth strategy, you create a
ripple effect, encouraging others to do the same.

Sparkle 10 Growth Tasks: Dealing with Negativity and Staying Positive

1. **Create a Positive Mantra:** Develop a personal mantra or affirmation that you can repeat to yourself when negativity arises. Examples: "I am confident in my voice," or "Other people's opinions don't define my worth." Write it down somewhere visible or save it as your phone wallpaper to remind yourself daily.

2. **Respond with Kindness:** The next time you receive a negative or critical comment, challenge yourself to respond calmly and positively. Before replying, take a moment to breathe, reflect, and approach the situation with empathy. If it's a genuine critique, offer a solution; if it's negativity for the sake of it, respond with grace or delete if necessary.

3. **Unfollow or Mute Accounts that Trigger Comparison:** Go through your social media following list and identify any accounts that consistently make you feel "less than." It could be that the content doesn't align with your values or triggers self-doubt. Don't hesitate to unfollow or mute these accounts to protect your mental well-being.

4. **Write a Gratitude List:** Reflect on what you've achieved so far in your journey. Write down at least five things you're grateful for about your

personal growth or the positive impact you've had on your community. Keep this list somewhere easy to access, so you can look back on it whenever comparison or negativity starts to creep in.

5. **Set Boundaries for Screen Time**: Schedule regular breaks from social media to recharge and refresh. Create a plan for how often you'll take "digital detox" days or even a few hours away from the screen. During these breaks, focus on activities that nourish your mind and body, such as exercise, reading, or spending time with loved ones.

6. **Celebrate Small Wins**: Identify a recent accomplishment, no matter how small, and share it with your audience or journal about it. Shifting focus to positive achievements helps maintain a healthy mindset and reinforces the impact you're having, despite any negative feedback.

7. **Turn Off Notifications**: If the constant buzz of notifications makes you feel anxious or overwhelmed, set aside specific times during the day to check social media instead of being constantly plugged in. This helps you stay in control of your online engagement rather than being reactive to every comment or message.

8. **Start a Positivity Journal**: At the end of each day, write down one positive interaction or

piece of feedback you received. It could be a compliment, a kind comment, or a personal milestone. On tough days, revisit your positivity journal to remind yourself of all the good your content brings into the world.

Sparkle 11: Evolving as an Influencer – Growth Beyond the Numbers

Once you find a system that works for you, it feels incredible. That sense of flow, where things click, and social media magic seems to unfold with ease, is unmatched. The routine becomes familiar, and you know how to handle the day-to-day tasks that once seemed daunting. But then, like clockwork, an unexpected lull sets in, or you notice a subtle decline in engagement. Perhaps your energy isn't what it once was, or you're not as motivated to show up. This is often the most challenging part of any growth journey: the need to shift, grow, and adapt when you're already comfortable.

I'm a huge advocate for planning and systems – they bring so much value and stability to our workflows, and they work! But in social media, as in life, nothing stays static. Social media is dynamic, a constantly changing landscape where trends shift quickly and algorithms update regularly. What worked six months ago might feel out of date now, and what's popular today might be irrelevant tomorrow. We're working in an environment where adapting to change isn't just helpful – it's essential.

Social media has become almost unrecognizable from what it was just two or three years ago, and if we look back a decade, it feels like comparing the digital age to the dinosaur era. With this rapid evolution, I've intentionally chosen to keep platform-specific advice to a minimum in this book. Instead, I want to focus on branding, self-care, and personal growth principles that can stand the test of time. Who knows? Perhaps down the line, I'll release a "2.0" version of this book to keep up with new trends. And if you're looking for more current advice, you can always find me on social media at @sparkleandgrow for day-to-day updates.

Adapting to change is not just important—it's vital to thriving in the ever-evolving digital space. Trends and platform features will come and go, and if you're not actively adjusting, you may find yourself losing relevance before you even realize it. However, it's important to remember that while adaptation and evolution are necessary, they don't require you to change the foundation of your brand. Your core identity and values remain constant, acting as your anchor. The shifts you make should center around creative expression, such as experimenting with new content styles or leveraging emerging platform features, rather than altering the heart of your message. This is why there's no need to stress about change—when your foundation is solid, the adjustments you make will be opportunities to innovate and grow, not overhaul your identity.

Recognizing When to Pivot

So, how can you tell when it's time to make a change? The signs are often there if you know where to look. Start with your metrics. Pay attention to trends like declining engagement rates (likes, comments, shares), reduced reach, or a noticeable dip in click-through rates. These numbers don't just measure popularity – they're feedback on how well your content aligns with your audience's current interests and needs.

Engagement trends are especially revealing. Are your audience interactions slowing down, or do comments feel less meaningful? For instance, if your posts used to spark in-depth conversations but now only gather a few emojis, it might indicate a disconnect. Additionally, compare the performance of different types of content. If certain formats (like reels, carousels, or stories) consistently outperform others, consider leaning more into what's working.

Beyond the numbers, pay attention to indirect feedback. Are people saving your posts or sending direct messages about your content? These quieter actions often indicate deeper value. Look at your follower behavior too. If you're gaining followers but not retaining them, it could mean your content isn't meeting expectations after that initial click. Use tools like audience retention graphs in video analytics to see where people drop off, and dig into those moments.

But metrics aren't the whole story. Sometimes, the signal comes from within. If the passion that once fueled you feels more like a chore, it might not mean the idea itself has failed – it could mean you're in the "honeymoon phase hangover." In the beginning, it's normal to be swept up in excitement, but sustaining that energy requires new sparks of creativity. Ask yourself: *Is the concept still meaningful to me, or have I outgrown it?* If the passion is still there, focus on ways to reinvigorate your connection to your work. Experiment with fresh ideas, collaborate with other creators, or take a short break to regain perspective.

When considering a pivot, balance intuition with evidence. Look for patterns, not just one-off anomalies. A single underperforming post doesn't warrant an overhaul, but consistent underperformance across a theme or style might. Also, recognize the difference between temporary trends and consistent interests. Trend-based content may bring quick wins, but lasting success comes from aligning your brand with what you genuinely care about and what consistently resonates with you and your audience. Also, know that if you do choose to shift your topics it's normal to see a dip for a while before you see some growth again. It's your audience shifting with you - some of your previous fans may or may not connect with your new topics, but eventually another niche of audience will build that *is* interested in the new topics.

Lastly, give yourself permission to adapt. The most successful creators aren't afraid to evolve when necessary. A pivot doesn't mean failure – it's a sign of growth and responsiveness. Stay curious about your audience, your analytics, and your own creative journey, and you'll find the path that keeps you both inspired and aligned with your goals.

Keeping Changes Aligned with Your Long-Term Vision

When you do make these shifts, remember that every tweak should stay true to your overarching vision and brand. This is where the importance of having a clearly defined "why" and personal brand shines. Knowing your purpose and goals helps you determine where to pivot and where to hold steady. A strong brand foundation enables you to recognize which trends align with your purpose and which might dilute your message.

Branding yourself and defining your "why" keeps you focused on what truly matters. It's easy to get caught up in momentary trends or feel pressured to replicate what's working for others. But if a shift doesn't feel authentic, it's probably not worth it. The beauty of a solid personal brand is that it keeps you grounded –

it's like a compass pointing you toward what aligns with your values and goals, regardless of external pressures.

Building a Sustainable, Impactful Brand

As we've been learning, alignment creates a foundation that supports consistent, meaningful content. A sustainable personal brand isn't just about keeping up with what's trending; it's about finding what resonates with your audience and building a space they want to return to. People should feel at home when they visit your page, whether they've been following you for years or stumbled upon you for the first time. Consistency in your values and message builds trust and keeps people coming back, fostering a loyal community that values your voice and perspective.

And this loyalty isn't just emotionally fulfilling – it can lead to financial success. When you serve your audience authentically, when your content reflects genuine care and passion, people notice. They're more likely to support you by purchasing your products, engaging with sponsored content, or simply being your most dedicated followers. This kind of loyalty is invaluable and positions you for long-term, sustainable growth.

Embracing the Evolution Process: Staying Relevant with Purpose

Flexibility and self-reflection are not just important—they're essential. As the digital landscape shifts, so must your approach to staying relevant while remaining true to your brand. Growth as an influencer isn't only about increasing numbers or followers; it's about deepening your understanding of your purpose and consistently refining how you deliver value to your audience.

But what does that look like in practice? Let's explore the art of evolving your brand while maintaining its authenticity.

How to Spot Trends that Matter

In a world where trends seem to pop up daily, it's tempting to jump on every bandwagon. However, not every trend aligns with your purpose or resonates with your audience. Here's how to navigate this:

1. **Follow Industry Leaders and Trend Reports**
   Keep tabs on creators and brands within your niche. Tools like Google Trends, TikTok's "For You" page, and social media listening platforms can provide insight into emerging trends.
2. **Observe Audience Behavior**
   Watch for shifts in the type of content your

audience engages with. For example, are they saving more carousel posts, commenting on authentic storytelling reels, or sharing content that's humorous or educational? These patterns can reveal emerging preferences.

3. **Test Before Committing**
   Dip your toes into trends before fully adopting them. Try creating a piece of content that aligns with a trend but stays true to your brand voice and see how your audience responds.

Deciding If a Trend Aligns with Your Brand

Once you identify a trend, the next step is determining whether it fits your purpose. Here are a few questions to help guide you:

- **Does this trend complement my brand values?**
  For example, if you promote wellness and positivity, a sarcastic or edgy trend might not resonate with your audience. Instead, adapt the trend in a way that aligns with your message.
- **Can I make this trend my own?**
  Authenticity comes from putting your unique spin on what's popular. For instance, if a trending audio clip feels overused, add a personal anecdote or a surprising twist to make it fresh.
- **Will it serve my audience?**
  If a trend doesn't add value or entertain in a

meaningful way, it may not be worth pursuing. Always consider what your audience stands to gain from the content.

Staying Relevant While Staying True

To remain relevant in a constantly evolving space, focus on marrying current trends with your foundational purpose. This balance allows you to grow without losing sight of what makes your brand unique.

Examples of Staying Relevant

1. **Transformational Hashtags:**
   If #MondayMotivation trends and your brand centers around personal growth, creating a post showcasing your weekly rituals or encouraging followers to set intentions. Tie the trend back to your core content pillars.
2. **Creative Visuals:**
   When bold graphics or specific video transitions become trendy, adopt the visual style to make your content pop, but pair it with captions or themes that feel uniquely you.
3. **Interactive Content:**
   Trends like polls, Q&A stickers, or viral challenges can become tools to deepen community engagement. Use them to ask your audience questions related to your niche or invite them to share their own stories.

Practical Tips for Trend-Adoption

1. **Start Small with One Trend at a Time**
   Avoid overwhelming yourself by trying to
   tackle multiple trends. Instead, choose one that
   aligns well and experiment with different ways
   to incorporate it into your content.
2. **Batch-Test Ideas**
   Create a few variations of content around the
   same trend to see which resonates most. For
   instance, film a lighthearted take, a more
   serious version, and one that's purely
   educational.
3. **Stay Open to Feedback**
   Pay attention to comments, shares, and direct
   messages. Your audience's response will tell
   you whether the trend connects or feels out of
   place.

The Dynamic Between Consistency and Evolution

Remember: while trends are fleeting, your brand
identity is the constant. Consistency doesn't mean
stagnation; it means always bringing your unique
perspective, voice, and style to the table. Evolution
doesn't mean losing your essence; it's about finding
fresh ways to express it.

Building a System for Trend-Adaptive Content

- **Content Pillars as a Compass**
  Your content pillars are your guiding stars.
  Before embracing any trend, ask yourself how
  it fits into your core themes. If your pillars are
  mindset, wellness, and authenticity, trends
  should feed into one or more of these
  categories.
- **Scheduling Trend-Based Content**
  Create a "trend slot" in your posting schedule.
  For example, allocate one post per week to
  explore current trends while keeping the rest
  aligned with evergreen content.

Evolving Without Losing Your Roots

Each adjustment and pivot you make contributes to
the evolution of your personal brand, bringing you
closer to the ideal version of what you want to create.
Embrace change, but stay true to your *why*. By
intentionally connecting trends to your core values
and purpose, you'll ensure that your growth feels
authentic both to you and your audience.

For example:

- A health coach adapting a viral dance trend
  might showcase it as part of their morning
  fitness routine.

- A DIY creator could align a trending color palette with their latest crafting tutorial.

The possibilities are endless when you view trends as tools rather than distractions. Serve the world with authenticity, and the good vibes and bright light you put out will undoubtedly be returned to you.

Sparkle 11 Growth Tasks: Evolving as an Influencer

1. **Reflect on Your Why**
   Take 5–10 minutes to revisit your core mission
   and vision. Write down the purpose that drives
   your online presence and any recent changes in
   your passions or interests. This will ground you
   and keep your future adjustments aligned with
   your goals.

2. **Audit Your Content**
   Review your recent posts, stories, or videos.
   Identify what's resonating with your audience
   and what's not. Pay attention to both
   engagement metrics and audience feedback to
   pinpoint areas for improvement or potential
   shifts in your content.

3. **Experiment with Small Changes**
   Choose one small adjustment to try over the
   next week. This could be tweaking your posting
   time, adding new visual styles, or
   experimenting with a different tone. Track the
   results to see how this small change impacts
   engagement.

4. **Check Your Analytics Regularly**
   Set a schedule to review your analytics –
   whether weekly or monthly. Look at metrics
   like reach, impressions, and engagement. Use
   these insights to spot trends or shifts that
   might indicate it's time for a strategic pivot.

5. **Engage in Ongoing Learning**
    Commit to staying updated on social media
    trends and best practices. Subscribe to a
    podcast, join a relevant group, or follow
    industry leaders. Keeping a pulse on the
    industry will help you anticipate shifts and stay
    agile.

6. **Ask Your Audience for Feedback**
    Poll your audience or ask open-ended questions
    in your stories to find out what they'd love to
    see more of. This helps you stay connected to
    their evolving interests and keeps your content
    valuable and relevant.

7. **Reaffirm Your Brand Consistency**
    Review your social media bio, profile picture,
    and highlights. Make sure these align with your
    brand's current tone and message, creating a
    cohesive experience that feels familiar to new
    and returning followers.

8. **Celebrate Small Wins and Adjustments**
    Take time to recognize the small improvements
    and milestones you achieve, no matter how
    minor. This helps you stay motivated,
    appreciate your progress, and embrace change
    with a positive mindset.

Sparkle 12: Conclusion – Sparkle, Grow, and Shine

Omgeeee—you've made it to the last chapter! That's how I feel reaching the final stretch of a book; it's like crossing the finish line on a marathon of learning. This might seem like the typical wrap-up, but I dare you to spend extra time here. You've put in serious work throughout this book, and now we're focusing on a deep reflection of your personal and professional growth. If you've been following along and doing the activities, the progress you've made should be remarkable by now. Think of this as a pause to breathe, appreciate, and prepare for your next steps.

This isn't just a "read once and done" book. *Sparkle and Grow* is meant to be a long-term resource—a book you can keep revisiting. Each chapter offers you insights to lean on and refresh at different stages of your journey. Maybe today you resonate most with personal wellness, and a few months from now, brand strategy becomes your focus. Keep this book close; as you evolve, so will your understanding and approach to these topics. You'll find that different elements of the book will shine brighter depending on where you are in your journey.

Embrace Your Journey

The road to building an authentic brand is as unique as each person reading this. This book wasn't about telling you to mimic someone else's success. This has been about uncovering your distinct qualities, the things that make you unapologetically *you*. You've discovered that authenticity, self-love, and growth are essential, but let's be real: it's not going to be flawless. However, it will be worth it. Every misstep or challenge becomes a lesson that adds depth to your journey. So, let yourself be proud of the process because this is what will set you apart.

Every day you show up as yourself, you're building a brand that resonates deeply with your audience. Take pride in your growth and enjoy every step—it's a journey that's meant to be lived fully.

Set Actionable Goals

Setting goals gives you a reason to celebrate milestones, both big and small, along the way. Take a moment here and now to define three goals: one for personal growth, one for your brand, and one for mental wellness. Writing these down helps to solidify them, and as you reach each one, you'll build momentum and confidence.

Set three intentional goals that excite and motivate you. These small actions add up, so don't shy away from taking them one step at a time.

Prioritize Your Well-Being

Success should feel as good as it looks. Burnout, on the other hand, is the surest way to feel disconnected from the joy of creating. Prioritizing your wellness is non-negotiable; make self-care part of your weekly routine, whether it's meditation, journaling, or simply disconnecting to recharge.

True success happens when you nurture your mind and body. Take intentional breaks to rejuvenate so that you can show up fully for your audience and yourself.

Build an Authentic Community

Creating a brand is also about creating relationships, which means more than just "likes" and "follows." It's about showing up genuinely, caring about your followers, and creating a space where they feel valued. This depth is where true influence lives.

Spend a few minutes each day engaging with your community. Ask questions, respond thoughtfully, and make those connections meaningful.

Embrace Growth and Adaptation

There's no such thing as staying the same, especially in this world. Growth often comes with shifts and pivots—embrace them. Look at each change as an opportunity to expand your brand in a new direction, stay curious, and welcome learning.

Be open to where this journey takes you. Growth isn't a straight line, but every twist and turn is building a foundation for long-term success.

Take the Next Step with Confidence

By now, you have the tools, confidence, and direction to go after what you want. It's time to put it all into practice, to push yourself out of your comfort zone and explore the opportunities waiting for you. Launch that project, share that story, reach out for that collaboration—take the leap!

Confidence comes from knowing you're prepared. Take that step toward your dream, and trust that you have what it takes to make it happen.

Reflect on Your 'Why'

Remember your 'why' like a guiding light. As you achieve new milestones, it's easy to get swept up in numbers and comparisons. Revisit your core purpose often to stay grounded in what truly matters.

When you stay connected to your why, your brand becomes a natural extension of yourself. It's your compass for authenticity.

Continue the Conversation

Lastly, this is just the beginning! I'd love to stay connected and hear about your journey, so don't hesitate to reach out. Join the online community at sparkleandgrow.com or on social media platforms via @sparkleandgrow, sign up for updates, or simply follow along so we can keep learning and supporting each other on this journey.

This path is yours to define, but you're not alone on it. Let's keep the energy going—connect, share, and continue to sparkle and grow with a community that's cheering you on.

And with that, you're ready to go out and *sparkle, grow, and shine* with confidence, creativity, and courage! This journey doesn't end here; it's only beginning. Let this be the book you revisit when you need that extra push. The world's waiting for you—now go and shine your light!